THE

ANOINTING OF
PRESERVATION

Destiny Image Books by Hank Kunneman

The Supernatural Power of Jesus' Blood

Throne Room Prophecy

My Heart Cries Abba

The Prayer from the Crypt

Barrier Breakers

Spiritual A.D.D.

Comic Books

Galactic Quests of Captain Zepto:

The Island of Doom

Disturbance in the Galaxy

The Cosmic Inflation

The Christmas Cane Caper

The Great Z-Clips

Children's Books

The Adventures of Mutzphey and Milo

Mutzphey's Last Stand

The Teacher's Pet

Treehouse SSO

Mutzphey's Longest Day

HANK KUNNEMAN

THE

ANOINTING OF
PRESERVATION

LIVING SUPERNATURALLY
SHIELDED FROM THE
POWERS OF DARKNESS

DESTINY IMAGE® PUBLISHERS, INC.
PO Box 310, Shippensburg, PA 17257-0310

"Publishing cutting-edge prophetic resources to supernaturally empower the body of Christ"

This book and all other Destiny Image and Destiny Image Fiction books are available at Christian bookstores and distributors worldwide.

For more information on foreign distributors, call 717-532-3040.

Reach us on the Internet: www.destinyimage.com.

ISBN 13 TP: 978-0-7684-6480-1

ISBN 13 eBook: 978-0-7684-6481-8

For Worldwide Distribution, Printed in the USA

1 2 3 4 5 6 7 8 / 27 26 25 24 23

CONTENTS

INTRODUCTION

As believers, we have been anointed with a special gift from God—the power of preservation!

This book will bring you closer to understanding and unlocking your potential through this precious endowment. We can use it not only for self-preservation but also as spiritual armor against evil forces seeking to keep us down. Let's revel in this loving protection God has for us and be awakened by its ability to lift our spirits. Allow it to expand your knowledge about what comes with the *Anointing of Preservation!*

Get ready to experience the spiritual realm of God's anointing and witness its supernatural effects on relationships, politics, households, and nations! Let these words guide you toward the divine protection that God has even for your life.

There were many attempts to kill Jesus prematurely while He was on this earth. This same anointing of preservation kept Him alive until He was ready to lay down His life and be crucified.

It's time to reclaim what was promised! Jesus was preserved by the anointing of God, but that same power resides in each one of us too. I'm passionate about sharing His truth with you—so get ready for a life-changing revelation as we dive into understanding how the incredible *Anointing of Preservation* can unleash your journey to living more abundantly!

1

PRESERVATION IS PROTECTION

*It shall come to pass in that day, that his burden shall be taken away from off thy shoulder, and his yoke from off thy neck, and the yoke shall be destroyed because of **the anointing** (Isaiah 10:27 KJV).*

I've been longing to write a book on the anointing for years now. It's my passion and I can't wait for you to experience the incredible benefits of this precious anointing. But what exactly is the anointing, you might ask? It's a divine equipping that allows ordinary people to achieve supernatural results. It's the power of God working through people, enabling them to do something extraordinary. The anointing is also God on human flesh, doing what human flesh can't do outside of this heavenly endowment. Just look at Jesus—when He was anointed with the Holy Spirit, His whole ministry was filled with supernatural occurrences.

The word *anointing* can also be defined as *anoint*, which means to rub into or smear something on. Jesus was smeared with the anointing of the Holy Spirit, and that's what made His ministry so extraordinary. So, let's seek the Holy Spirit and His anointing and watch as it empowers us to do incredible things for the glory of God. The anointing is not just for a select few believers—it's available to all who seek it. When we are anointed, we are equipped with the power and presence of the Holy Spirit to do the work of God in a mighty way. It's not about us, it's about the power of God working through us.

So how do we receive the anointing? It starts with a desire and a willingness to be used by God. We must humble ourselves and be obedient to His leading. As we draw near to God and seek His will, He will pour out His anointing upon us. And what can we expect when we are anointed? Miracles, signs, and wonders will follow, and the anointing that preserves will be the results. The anointing breaks the yoke of bondage and sets us free to walk in the fullness of all that God has for us. It brings healing to the sick and deliverance to the captives. It's a powerful force that cannot be denied.

So, let's pursue the anointing with all our hearts. Let's seek the face of God and ask Him to anoint us for His glory. And let's watch as He works through us in miraculous ways, bringing hope and healing to a lost and hurting world. The anointing is a force to be reckoned with. It can break yokes and lift heavy burdens, as we see in Isaiah 10:27.

But what exactly is a yoke? It's something that puts someone, a city, or a nation under the control of the enemy. It's like being a prisoner, unable to do what you want or go where you please. We see an example of a yoke in Acts 12:6, where Peter is imprisoned and bound with TWO chains, guarded by soldiers at the prison door. The only thing that could free Peter's destiny was divine intervention—and that's exactly what the anointing does. In verse 7, an angel of the Lord comes and sets Peter free, his chains falling off his hands.

In my studies and experience, I've come to realize that the anointing isn't just about the power of God working through us, it also serves as a protective shield in the battles and attacks of the enemy. This protection is known as the anointing of preservation.

But what is preservation? It's protection. It's God watching over us and making sure that nothing of the enemy can harm us. And through His anointing, God has made this protection available to us. The anointing serves as a seal of the Holy Spirit on our lives, a seal of His protection (Ephesians 1:13). So, let's seek the anointing and rest assured that as we walk in it, we are covered and protected by the mighty hand of God.

To understand the power of the anointing to preserve our lives, just think of an ox with a yoke on its shoulders. That ox is under the control, weight, and burden of that yoke. That's why the anointing is so powerful in the life of the believer—it destroys those yokes and undoes heavy burdens, no matter the pressures, challenges, or attacks of the enemy. Just imagine for a moment what it would be like to have that yoke taken away and destroyed/obliterated by the anointing. The results would be a life blessed by the Lord and protected from the enemy's attacks, a life that is full and abundant, just as Jesus promised in John 10:10.

I want to encourage you to always remember that it is the anointing that destroys the yokes that the enemy tries to ensnare us with. Some translations may say that the anointing breaks these yokes, but it's important to understand that the anointing *destroys* them. Why is this distinction important? Because if you can break something, it can potentially be put back together. But if you destroy something, it's damaged beyond repair, scattered beyond recovery, annihilated.

That's why the correct interpretation of Isaiah 10 is that the anointing destroys the yoke, not just breaks it. When the yoke is destroyed by the power of God, it will be in so many pieces that it can never be put back together again, never again serving as a burden or bond. Isaiah 10:27 (KJV) says, *"And it shall come to pass in that day, that his burden shall be taken away from off thy shoulder, and his yoke from off thy neck, and the yoke shall be destroyed because of the anointing."*

In Hebrew it is referring to the "fatness of the oxen," meaning prosperity and abundance that will come to the people of God because of the anointing destroying the yokes of bondage and lifting the heavy burdens. The fatness of the oxen symbolizes the abundance and prosperity that will be enjoyed by God's people when they are freed from their burdens and able to live in the fullness of all that God has for them. (I'll have more on this when I talk about your words.) This can include physical blessings such as provision and protection, as well as spiritual blessings such as joy, peace, and purpose. So when we seek the anointing and allow it to work in our lives, we can expect to experience not only freedom from bondage but also abundance and prosperity in every area of our lives.

That's the power of the anointing—it removes burdens and destroys the yokes of anything the enemy tries to entangle us with. And it's not just for annihilating yokes—it's also available to protect and preserve our very lives.

So how does this verse in Isaiah about a yoke correspond with the anointing of preservation or protection for us today? Well, just like in ancient times, the anointing is still here to destroy the yokes of bondage and set us free. But it also serves as a shield, protecting us from the attacks of the enemy and preserving our lives. This is why it is imperative to press for the anointing and experience the freedom and protection it brings.

YOUR WORDS ARE POWERFUL.

I want to show you just how powerful this anointing of preservation is, and how our words play a key role in activating and maintaining it in our lives. Just look at the life of Jesus. When He began His ministry, He declared with His words in the temple that the Spirit of the Lord God was upon Him (Luke 4:18). This was a decree backed by Heaven that released the anointing upon Him and preserved Him through temptations and attacks from the enemy, even to the point of death.

In the same way, by understanding this anointing of preservation and speaking words of faith, we can also be protected from the challenges and attacks of the devil in our life. This anointing is powerfully activated as preservation when we speak words of faith, knowing that we are protected and preserved by the power of God.

This announcement from Jesus was a powerful decree that activated the anointing of preservation upon His life, and it's the key for us today as well. From that moment forward in the temple, the anointing rested upon Jesus and preserved His life until He would lay it down, even though there were several attempts to kill Him before His crucifixion.

Jesus's proclamation that He was anointed by the Father and filled with the Holy Spirit caused quite a stir in the temple that day. Everyone's attention was fixed on Jesus as their anger grew, eventually reaching a boiling point where they were determined to kill Him on the spot. But despite the rage of those around Him, Jesus was protected and preserved by the anointing of the Holy Spirit.

And all they in the synagogue, when they heard these things, were filled with wrath, and rose up, and thrust him out of the city, and led him unto the brow of the hill whereon their city was built, that they might cast him down headlong. But he passing through the midst of them went his way, and came down to Capernaum, a city of Galilee, and taught them on the sabbath days (**Luke 4:28-31 KJV**).

But even though they tried to kill Jesus, taking Him to the edge of a cliff to throw Him off, they couldn't do it. Was it just because it wasn't His time or how He was supposed to die? Of course, that was part of it, but it was also because of the anointing of preservation that He had just announced was upon Him.

This anointing stayed with Jesus even after several attempts on His life, as we see in the book of John:

Therefore the Jews sought the more to kill him, because he not only had broken the sabbath, but said also that God was his Father, making himself equal with God (**John 5:18 KJV**).

After these things Jesus walked in Galilee: for he would not walk in Jewry, because the Jews sought to kill him (**John 7:1 KJV**).

Did not Moses give you the law, and yet none of you keepeth the law? Why go ye about to kill me? The people answered and said, Thou hast a devil: who goeth about to kill thee? (**John 7:19-20 KJV**)

Then said some of them of Jerusalem, Is not this he, whom they seek to kill? (**John 7:25 KJV**)

Then they sought to take him: but no man laid hands on him, because his hour was not yet come (John 7:30 KJV).

I know that ye are Abraham's seed; but ye seek to kill me, because my word hath no place in you (John 8:37 KJV).

But now ye seek to kill me, a man that hath told you the truth, which I have heard of God: this did not Abraham (John 8:40 KJV).

Then took they up stones to cast at him: but Jesus hid himself, and went out of the temple, going through the midst of them, and so passed by (John 8:59 KJV).

Then the Jews took up stones again to stone him. Jesus answered them, Many good works have I shewed you from my Father; for which of those works do ye stone me? (John 10:31-32 KJV)

His disciples say unto him, Master, the Jews of late sought to stone thee; and goest thou thither again? (John 11:8 KJV)

Then from that day forth they took counsel together for to put him to death (John 11:53 KJV).

In every one of these instances, the anointing Jesus had declared in the temple remained with Him and even increased in the Garden of Gethsemane as He prayed. It was so strong on Him that when they tried to arrest Him, they were powerless to seize Him and fell backward (John 18:4).

In addition, the anointing of preservation was so strong upon Jesus that He performed a miracle on the spot (John 18:10). Peter, one of Jesus's disciples, tried to defend Jesus by cutting off the ear of the high priest's servant, Malchus. But Jesus ministering in the anointing, healed Malchus's ear, showing that He did not come to fight or defend Himself by violence, but rather to lay down His life willingly for the salvation of mankind.

But now it was time for Jesus to lay down His life, and the anointing lifted off of Him. This allowed them to arrest and crucify Him for the greater purposes of God and the redemption of mankind. This anointing of preservation in the same way is also available for you, for your city, and for the nations of the earth to protect and preserve from the hand of the enemy that seeks to establish a yoke of bondage. Just like Jesus that day in the temple, you can increase and release this anointing by making a declaration and decreeing that the Spirit of the Lord is upon you, your city, and the nations of the earth and that His anointing rests upon all of it.

By making a powerful decree as Jesus did, you can add the anointing of preservation to your life, as seen in Jesus's life and ministry. I encourage you to start declaring that the Spirit of the Lord is upon you, that you are anointed, and that this anointing preserves you from all evil. This is exactly what is promised in Psalm 121—that you will be preserved from all evil, and that your soul and your daily comings and goings will be protected by this anointing of preservation.

> *The Lord shall preserve thee from all evil: he shall preserve thy soul. The Lord shall preserve thy going out and thy coming in from this time forth, and even for evermore* **(Psalm 121:7-8 KJV).**

Don't underestimate the power of this anointing to keep you safe and secure, no matter what challenges or attacks may come your way. This is exactly what Psalm 103 says regarding being crowned or surrounded by His preservation. It is part of the benefits the Lord provides in covenant with Him through Jesus Christ. The word for "crowned" in this verse means to surround or to protect and preserve.

> *Who redeemeth thy life from destruction; who crowneth thee with lovingkindness and tender mercies* **(Psalm 103:4 KJV).**

So how do I activate this crowning or surrounding of His preservation? Use the power of your words to activate and maintain the anointing of preservation in your life and the lives of those around you. Speak words of faith and declare the presence and power of the Holy Spirit upon you and all that you are responsible for, and watch as the anointing works to protect and preserve you and those you love.

As we continue to explore the powerful effects and results of the anointing of preservation, let's take a closer look at Isaiah 10 and see how different Bible translations describe this anointing and how we can activate it in our lives. The following are a few different translations of this verse to consider:

> *On that day God will end the bondage of his people. He will break the yoke of slavery off their necks and destroy it as decreed* (Isaiah 10:27 Living Bible).

It's important to note that this translation says that the yoke of slavery is destroyed when it is decreed. In other words, it is put into motion or enforced by a decree. In the same way, when we decree what God has spoken and understand the power of our words, we can see the things that the enemy tries to enslave us with be destroyed. God freed His people from bondage through a decree and released an anointing to do it and preserve them. That's why I am so passionate about sharing the truth of the anointing of preservation with you in this book—so that you, too, can experience freedom and preservation in this life.

Now, let's consider another translation to better understand the blessings of walking in the anointing of preservation and how it protects us from attacks and strongholds.

In that day their burden will be lifted from your shoulders, their yoke from your neck; the yoke will be broken because you have grown so fat **(Isaiah 10:27 New International Version).**

The literal Hebrew meaning of the phrase *"because you have grown so fat"* in this verse is because of the fatness. In the King James Version, it is translated as *"because of the anointing."* This is because the anointing brings fatness to our lives, meaning blessings, prosperity, supernatural power, and also preservation. So the true definition of this verse refers to the anointing as fatness that causes yokes to be destroyed because we have grown fat in the blessings of our covenant with God.

This spiritual fatness is exactly what happens when the anointing of preservation is upon our lives. It causes the enemy's attempts to ensnare us to be destroyed. As mentioned at the beginning of this chapter, imagine the fatness of an ox and what would happen when trying to put a yoke upon its shoulders. The yoke would break and be destroyed by the mere size or fatness and strength of the ox! The same is true with the anointing of preservation upon our lives when we decree it and walk in it. Yokes are utterly destroyed, and heavy burdens are removed!

This verse tells us that as God's anointed oxen, we are so strong and blessed that the fatness, prosperity, and strength that come from this anointing will destroy any and every yoke. They will never be put together against us again! It is this anointing of preservation that protects and preserves our lives because the yokes of the enemy cannot prosper against us and weigh us down with heavy burdens in this life, like with the oxen. When God's anointing is on us, we are preserved and protected. There is no yoke holding us back and no weapon can prosper or touch us. And here's the great part—the same is true for you and me!

Are you ready, as this verse mentions, to have burdens lifted off your shoulders, yokes destroyed by the anointing, and to walk and live in the anointing of preservation? Then we must do as Jesus did and start by declaring that the Spirit of the Lord is upon us, anointing us with the anointing of preservation. Remember, it is the anointing that preserves life—not just any life, but your life as well.

A NATIONAL YOKE

I have come to realize that the anointing of preservation is not just for personal protection, it can also cover entire cities and nations! Let's look at once again the verse in Isaiah regarding the anointing and how it destroys yokes when it is decreed.

> *On that day God will end the bondage of his people. He will break the yoke of slavery off their necks and destroy it as decreed* (Isaiah 10:27 Living Bible).

Notice in this verse that it is not just speaking in context of personal preservation only but in addition, a national yoke. This means we can pray and decree preservation, protection and blessings over our cities and nations. It is not just a personal preservation but activating the Lord's anointing to preserve on a bigger scale locally, regionally, and nationally.

We see this in the story of Israel and how God preserved them through a prophetic anointing.

> *And by a prophet the Lord brought Israel out of Egypt, and by a prophet was he preserved* (Hosea 12:13 KJV).

The anointing of preservation was clearly evident in the pillar of cloud by day and His fire by night that preserved the entire nation of Israel. If they stayed close to the Lord, this divine preservation went with them, protecting them from their enemies. We too can bring this anointing of preservation over our lives and our nation when we stay close to God and bless our nation with powerful words and decrees (Psalm 145:20).

And not only can the anointing of preservation protect our personal lives and our nation, it can also cover our cities. Proverbs 11:11 (NKJV) tells us that *"By the blessing of the upright the city is exalted, but it is overthrown by the mouth of the wicked."*

Consider how the Lord's blessing and protection have preserved the nation, yet it has been overthrown by the words and actions of evil people. This should serve as a warning to us about the importance of our words in this life, especially when we're speaking over our cities and nations. When we speak powerful Scriptures, prophetic promises, and decrees over our cities, God promises blessings along with preservation. Consider how powerful it is for us to pray for Jerusalem's peace, as an example. When we do, we are decreeing and expecting God to preserve Jerusalem through His peace.

If there was anything wrong with seeking spiritual benefit from prayer for Israel's well-being (peace), then why would such a thing exist? This is why we are encouraged by God to pray for the city of Jerusalem's peace. We can see that this beautiful city is protected thanks to God's peace when we seek His aid, asking for His peace to preserve it and the people. In the same way, it works for our nation and cities as well!

When we stand in faith and declare the Spirit of the Lord upon our nation, we are releasing the anointing of God upon it. This anointing will preserve our nation, protect it from the schemes of the enemy, and bless it with prosperity. We can see the evidence of this in the resilience of the United States throughout its history, despite the many challenges and obstacles it has faced. That is not to say this nation is perfect by any means or exclusive from God's chastisement. Rather, it is something that is in the very foundation of our nation when it was dedicated to the Lord God!

Just as the Lord preserved Israel and other nations, He will continue to preserve and protect the United States as we stand in faith and declare His presence and power upon it. So let us not be afraid to speak out, to decree and declare the anointing of preservation upon our nation, cities, and lives. When we do, we are activating the power of God to protect and bless us, and to overcome any obstacle or enemy that may try to come against us. I am convinced no matter how much evil tries to yoke us with a demonic agenda, legislation, or any other thing that would try to enslave us here in the United States, it won't ultimately succeed.

I am convinced that whatever plots may be launched against this nation—the United States of America—will ultimately fail. God spoke to me through a prophetic word that He gave me on August 16, 2020, revealing that He has placed an anointing of preservation upon this nation. He said that there would be an attempt to steal the outcome of the election, even delay it through a planned chaotic thing. He revealed in that prophetic word that ultimately, no matter what they would try to do, this nation would be preserved. God said, "Do you think they can steal My nation, the United States, from Me and the future generations of your children?" This is why I do not believe anyone can steal this nation from our loving God. Even the attempt to steal the outcome of our elections or to delay them through chaos, will not succeed. God's hand of protection is upon this nation. We must continue to stand firm in our faith and trust in His plans and purposes for America.

When God said, "Do you think anyone can steal My nation from Me?" it caused me to dive even deeper into studying the anointing, especially when it is connected to divine preservation. The Lord showed me that no matter the challenges or threats faced by our nation, ultimately at this time, it would be protected and preserved by His power and grace. He declared that He had placed a blessing on this country and that the prayers of His people would sustain it.

The founders of our nation had built upon a foundation of righteousness, and the anointing of preservation was embedded within it. Some 250 years later, the USA with its many challenges will rise again despite the ever-increasing political angst, gas prices and inflation, and cultural and social madness to name a few.

So, I thank God for the anointing of preservation; for without it, our nation would already be cited in the history books alongside other collapsed societies including the Roman Empire and China's Ming Dynasty.

GOD'S ANOINTING OF PRESERVATION IS ON THE UNITED STATES.

I firmly believe no matter what is mandated or shoved at us, the attempt to yoke us will fall apart by those who have plotted evil and become proponents of the devil's plan to try to destroy our country. No matter how crazy the culture gets, or even as evil people try their wicked agenda, there is an anointing that God has purposely put upon this nation to counter it, preserving it for the final harvest. With the anointing of preservation upon us, we can experience a great awakening in which masses come to Jesus to be saved and wickedness is overturned.

This is possible because of the prayers of believers who have called out to God for His intervention and the release of His powerful hand and Spirit of preservation. Through this anointing, we can see powerful reforms take place in our lives, cities, and nations, as everything it touches is affected by the transformative power of God.

A PHYSICAL YOKE

Have you ever stopped to consider the importance of your own life in the grand scheme of things? You are a precious child of God, and He has a plan for your life that is greater than you can imagine. He wants to preserve you and bless you so that you can bring glory to His name and touch the lives of others in a powerful, supernatural way.

But know this: the devil is threatened by you and will attack you at every turn. He knows that you have the anointing of the Holy Spirit of preservation upon you, and he will do everything possible to try and bring you down. This is why you may have faced hardships and struggles in your life—it's because the enemy is fighting against you with great fear and fury.

But don't let him win! The devil is a defeated foe, so always remember that you are preserved by the covenant of Jesus's blood and the anointing of the Holy Spirit. Hold fast to your faith and trust in God and know that He has a mighty plan for your life. You are important to Him, and He will preserve you and your family, your health, your finances, and your future. You are an instrument of His glory, and He will use you to bless others and bring honor to His name.

The enemy is using all manner of tactics to try and place physical yokes on us with pain, sickness, and disease. He wants nothing more than to wear us down and enslave us to his will. But we must not forget the power that we have in Jesus Christ! When we declare, "The Spirit of the Lord God is upon me, He has anointed me," we are activating the preservation and protection that comes through the anointing of the Holy Spirit, just like we saw with Jesus.

Do not underestimate the impact of your words. When you speak the Word of God, you are destroying any hold that the enemy may try to have on you. Remember, you are preserved through the covenant of Jesus's blood, and the anointing of the Holy Spirit. Trust in the Lord and His power to protect and preserve you, both individually and globally, especially as we face pandemics and other challenges.

The truth is revealed in Scripture. In Isaiah 54:17 (NKJV) the Lord declares:

> *"**No weapon** formed against you shall prosper, and every tongue which rises against you in judgment you shall condemn. This is the heritage of the servants of the Lord, and their righteousness is from Me," says the Lord.*

As Christians, it is our heritage and our right to live in the blessing of God's anointing. Through the fatness of His covenant promise, we are protected and preserved by the power of the Holy Spirit. This means that we cannot be yoked or enslaved by the enemy. We are free in Christ, and we can walk in the fullness of His blessings and protection.

We can confidently declare, as the text essentially states, "Anxiety, you can't touch me. Sickness, you can't touch me!" When we understand that we have been anointed by God for preservation, we know that no weapon from the enemy can harm us. God's Word says that *"No weapon formed against you will prosper."* None. No weapon that the devil has formed against you will prosper. This is the protection and empowerment that the Holy Spirit brings to our lives through the anointing of preservation.

BECAUSE OF GOD'S ANOINTING, NO WEAPON WILL PROSPER.

We should boldly declare, "God says no weapon formed against me shall prosper, and I believe it!" God will condemn any tongue that rises against us, and we have the right and privilege as part of our heritage in Christ to also condemn it. It does not matter what others may say because our righteousness comes from Him. This is our heritage because Jesus paid for our salvation, or *sozo* in Greek, through His blood. Romans 10:13 (NKJV) states that *"whoever calls on* the name of the Lord shall be saved." And, "If you confess with your mouth the Lord Jesus and believe in your heart that God raised Him from the dead, you will be saved" [sozo] (Romans 10:9 NKJV).

When we ask Jesus to forgive our sins and be the Lord of our lives, we are saved according to Scripture. However, being saved is not just about forgiveness of sin only or receiving a mansion in Heaven and eternal life. It also includes many other benefits that can enrich and preserve our lives. These benefits, known as the *sozo* or full-benefits package, include preservation, protection, rescue, safety, prosperity, soundness of mind, deliverance, joy, peace, and long life. These are all given to us at the time of salvation when we call upon the name of the Lord.

YOU'RE ENTITLED TO THE FULL BENEFITS PACKAGE!

As believers, we must always remember that we have the right to declare that *no weapon formed against us will prosper* and to condemn any word that rises against us in judgment. This is because it is our covenant privilege and our right as recipients of salvation through Jesus Christ and His shed blood. The anointing of preservation is upon us and protects us from any adverse or harmful influences. You're preserved; it's part of the gift you received, and the anointing on your life.

2

THE ANOINTING
ACTIVATES
PRESERVATION

This anointing of preservation is crucial, and it is important to understand the power of the anointing. As mentioned at the beginning of this chapter, the anointing is the divine, supernatural power of God that comes upon human flesh to do what we are unable to do on our own.

Declaring that the anointing of the Spirit of God is upon our lives is important for many reasons, including the fact that it activates preservation.

Christians often talk about the works of God, saying things like, "Look at what God did," or, "God showed up today," or "God healed that person." But how is it that God can do these things? The answer lies in the importance of the anointing, which is the source of God's power and ability to work in our lives.

So he answered and said to me: "This is the word of the Lord to Zerubbabel: 'Not by might nor by power, but by My Spirit,'" says the Lord of hosts (Zechariah 4:6 NKJV).

According to the prophet Zechariah, what we accomplish is not the result of our strength or abilities, but rather it is the work of God's Spirit and His anointing. It is why the Scripture says, we *"can do all things through Christ who strengthens me"* (Philippians 4:13 NKJV). Notice, it mentions the word *Christ* as being the enabler. It is because this word means anointing and it is the Anointed Christ and His anointing that gives you the ability to do all things by His Spirit.

This anointing is like a calling or a set of skills given to us for a specific purpose. Jesus, who was fully God and fully human, was anointed to do the work that needed to be done on earth. Through His anointing, He was able to do things that were beyond the abilities of ordinary people. When we are saved, we also receive an anointing and, like on the day of Pentecost, we can be filled with the Holy Spirit, enabling us to do the work that God has called us to do with supernatural power!

__God anointed Jesus__ of Nazareth __with the Holy Spirit__ and with power, who went about doing good and healing all who were oppressed by the devil, for God was with Him (Acts 10:38 NKJV).

Jesus, who was fully God and fully man, was empowered by the Holy Spirit. The Holy Spirit enabled Jesus to do good and to heal those who were oppressed by the devil. Everything that Jesus did, including His actions, words, corrections, and confrontations, was considered good. It is important to understand that Jesus's anointing allowed Him to do good, including making corrections and engaging in confrontations. He didn't just engage the religious hierarchy of His day, but also those in the culture and even those in the political.

In the same way, we should not avoid or resist being politically involved or tackling controversial topics—Jesus did not always take a passive approach. For example, in Luke 13:31-32, Jesus told the Pharisees to go and tell the political leader Herod, *"Go, tell that fox..."* indicating that He was not afraid to confront those in positions of political power. Furthermore, as seen in these verses, Jesus wanted Herod to know that He would continue to do what His Father called Him to do, and He wasn't changing or adjusting to the political corrupt powers of the Roman government.

Why did Jesus say this to Herod? It was because He knew the anointing on His life not only empowered Him but preserved Him even from the effects of the corrupt Roman Empire. This anointing that rested on Jesus enabled Him, as well as stirring Him to speak out against the wrongs of His culture, even if it meant confronting the political establishment and leaders like Herod. As you can see in His ministry, Jesus did not shy away from addressing the issues of the day, including speaking out against the Roman government and the Pharisees. He made it clear that He would continue to heal the sick and cast out demons, regardless of what others thought or wanted.

Unfortunately, today many leaders are more concerned with pleasing others or conforming to the culture rather than standing up for what is right. However, as believers, we have been given the same anointing that Jesus had, which enables us to do good and speak out for truth and justice. This anointing is vital for the preservation of truth and the gospel, and for standing against evil and the works of the devil. It is our responsibility to use the anointing we have been given to speak up, speak out boldly, minister to those who are oppressed and stand for what is right, including culture and politics.

WHAT? DON'T GET POLITICAL? WELL, JESUS DID.

As we see from Jesus's encounter with Herod, He was not afraid to confront evil, sin, and immorality. Some scholars believe that Jesus's reference to Herod as a "fox" was a criticism of his immoral lifestyle and sexual perversion. It is important to remember that a nation, city, or people will not be preserved if we avoid confronting evil and darkness.

Part of the anointing that Jesus carried was to be bold and even confront the things that were harming the people He ministered to, including the political realm. This is an important aspect of going about doing good. Both Jesus and the apostles, such as Paul and Peter, were anointed to affect not just the religious community, but also the political hierarchy and establishments of their time. They did not cower from speaking out against injustice and wrongdoing.

John the Baptist and Jesus were both anointed to speak to the culture and confront sin, including in the political realm. John the Baptist even went so far as to confront Herod about his immoral lifestyle. As believers who are anointed by the Spirit of God and carry an anointing to preserve our cities and nations, it is important that we follow in the example of John the Baptist and Jesus by not being silent about evil, and by actively getting involved in doing good and confronting evil.

> *For Herod himself had sent and laid hold of John and bound him in prison for the sake of Herodias, his brother Philip's wife; for he had married her. Because John had said to Herod, "It is not lawful for you to have your brother's wife"* (Mark 6:17-18 NKJV).

It is not accurate to say that Christ's followers are not anointed to affect the political realm or that they should not involve religion with politics. John the Baptist's confrontation with Herod, serves as an example of the boldness and conviction with which believers should approach issues of sin and injustice, even in the political realm. John the Baptist was not simply trying to be nice when he confronted Herod; rather, he was following the guidance of the Spirit and standing up for what he believed was right. Similarly, Christ's followers today should not avoid addressing political issues or engaging with the political process when it is necessary to do so to promote righteousness and justice.

> But Herod the tetrarch, being rebuked by him concerning Herodias, his brother Philip's wife, and for all the evils which Herod had done, also added this, above all, that he shut John up in prison (Luke 3:19-20 NKJV).

This verse suggests that John the Baptist's confrontation with Herod was not a one-time occurrence, but rather an ongoing effort. The verse specifically mentions that John confronted Herod not only about his brother Philip's wife but "all the evils" that Herod had done. This ongoing confrontation and lists of evil corruption likely contributed to John being thrown in prison. It is possible that if John had not inserted himself into the situation—as some suggest that we should do today and stay out of politics—he may have been able to avoid being thrown in prison. However, it is also important to note that John was guided by his faith and the leading of the Holy Spirit and was willing to stand up for what he believed was right, even at personal cost.

Unfortunately, there are some individuals today who prioritize the preservation of their ministry over speaking out against corruption and injustice. These individuals stay quiet on important issues. They do this as they avoid subjects that could be controversial or uncomfortable for their church members, even if those issues relate to moral standards or involve corrupt politicians and legislation. By staying quiet, they miss the opportunity to tap into the anointing of preservation that Jesus and John the Baptist demonstrated, and they fail to bring needed reform to our culture. In doing so, they also fail to be a voice for their con-gregations, who may be seeking truth and guidance on difficult issues.

Remember, it was the shepherds whom the host of Heaven appeared to at the time of our Lord's birth, who were watching over their flocks by night. In the same way, pastors today must not only guide, feed, nurture, and pro-tect their congregations, but in addition, watch over them regarding the dark evils of the day in which they live. It is imperative that we have bold, brave pastors, leaders and believers. God needs those who are willing to stand up for truth, righteousness, and justice, even if it means risking their ministry or reputation, to bring freedom and share the gospel.

John the Baptist had a powerful anointing on his life and ministry, and he was not afraid to speak boldly and con-front sin and evil. Jesus even referred to the anointing on John as the spirit of Elijah, who was known for his boldness and confrontation of King Ahab, Jezebel, and the evil hap-pening in his day. Similarly, Jesus Himself was recognized as having this same anointing of bold confrontation. In Matthew 16, the disciples compared Jesus to two figures known for their boldness and confrontational spirit: John the Baptist and Elijah.

So they said, "Some say John the Baptist, some Elijah, and others Jeremiah or one of the prophets" (Matthew 16:14 NKJV).

This anointing of boldness and confrontation is an important aspect of the ministry of believers who are called to stand up for truth, righteousness, and justice in the face of evil.

I find it interesting that the people of Jesus's time compared Him to John the Baptist and Elijah. They mentioned their names first because both of these figures were known for their nonconformity, confrontation, and boldness in their message. This was also true of Jesus, who carried an anointing to do good and undo the works of the devil. Like John the Baptist and Elijah, Jesus was not afraid to confront sin and evil, and He stood up for truth and righteousness even in the face of opposition. Notice, all three of these men not only engaged the culture but confronted the political powers of their day. This nonconformity, confrontation, and boldness were all important aspects of the anointing that Jesus carried and the ministry that He fulfilled.

The anointing of the Holy Spirit was a key aspect of Jesus's ministry of doing good and confronting evil. This anointing was necessary for the preservation of good, truth, and moral living, especially during a time when the world was steeped in darkness. Jesus Himself described His ministry as a great light that appeared in the darkness, and this light was the anointing of preservation that would help to preserve Israel.

Today, we face many similar challenges as a nation, and we must follow the example of Jesus by actively confronting evil and working to promote righteousness and justice. We cannot simply leave everything to the secular world and hope that things will improve on their own; we must take an active role in seeking to preserve good and combat evil in our society.

When I refer to an anointing of preservation that is bold and confronting, when necessary, I am not suggesting that this means acting rude or obnoxious. I also do not mean to imply that Jesus did not walk in love when I mention that He was not "nice" in the sense of conformity. It is important to remember that love and kindness, as described in the Fruit of the Spirit (Galatians 5:22-23), do not necessarily mean being "nice" or conforming to others' expectations. Rather, they involve speaking the truth in love and acting in a loving, kind way that does not compromise biblical truths or standards. Jesus Himself exemplified this kind of love, but He was not afraid to confront sin and evil, when necessary, even if it meant standing up to those in positions of power or authority.

As part of the anointing that rested on Him, Jesus demonstrated a confronting love that spoke the truth against evil. For example, when the woman caught in adultery was being accused by the Pharisees, Jesus wrote in the sand, confronting the situation in a way that ultimately resulted in good. It is possible that He may have even been writing the names of those who had sinned with her. Throughout His ministry, Jesus went about doing good and healing all who were oppressed by the devil. It is important to recognize that the devil is the source of sickness and evil in the world, and it is our calling as believers to confront and oppose these forces through the power of the anointing of the Holy Spirit.

As believers, we are anointed to do the same works that Jesus did: doing good, ministering to the needs of others, and destroying the works of darkness. This is why it is so important for us to connect to the anointing, as it is the key to preservation and success in our lives. By connecting to the anointing and allowing it to guide and empower our actions, we can fulfill our calling to be agents of good in the world and make a positive impact in the lives of those around us.

Throughout the Bible, we see that those who received God's anointing and followed His principles were successful in their ministries and able to change the lives and communities around them. If you want your life or business to be successful, it is important to seek God's anointing and follow His principles. One way to do this is to tithe and give offerings to support God's Kingdom, and to put God first in everything you do. By maintaining honor in all that you do and actively seeking God's anointing, you can experience prosperity in your business and see your natural endeavors become supernaturally successful. It is also important to proclaim that you and your business are anointed, as this can help to manifest God's blessings in your life.

For many years, I have had the opportunity to prophesy over business owners and speak words of encouragement and guidance from the Lord that can help to unlock the supernatural blessings of God in their businesses. Some of the individuals I have spoken to have received these words and experienced the prophetic anointing being released because they applied supernatural biblical principles to the word they were given. However, not all of them have reaped the reward of this anointing. This may be due to not applying or receiving the anointing and word by honoring it in their actions and decisions. It is important to remember that to experience the full blessings of God's anointing, we must be receptive to His guidance and seek to honor it in our lives.

Some people may say, "Oh, I give hundreds (or thousands or millions) to charity." While it is commendable to give to charity, it is also important to consider whether you are connecting to the anointing in the things you give or connect to. If you have financial resources, you can seek out an anointed prophetic ministry or church to support. When you sow into these ministries and connect with the anointing, you can experience blessings in your business, family, relationships, and life because you are connecting to the highest blessings that exist, the Kingdom of God!

> *Lay not up for yourselves treasures upon earth, where moth and rust doth corrupt, and where thieves break through and steal: But lay up for yourselves treasures in heaven, where neither moth nor rust doth corrupt, and where thieves do not break through nor steal: For where your treasure is, there will your heart be also* **(Matthew 6:19-21 KJV).**

As we see in this passage of Scripture in Matthew chapter 6, by connecting to the anointing and following the anointed principle of sowing and reaping into the Kingdom of God, we can experience the greatest return blessing of anything that exists. As Jesus Himself said, our finances will be protected from moths, rust, and thieves when we connect to the anointing of preservation.

It may be tempting in these times to focus on storing up for a rainy day, but this approach does not offer the same level of preservation as connecting to the anointing. James, the elder brother of Jesus, expands upon this teaching in his writings, further emphasizing the importance of connecting our lives and finances to the anointing to experience the full blessings of God.

Go to now, ye rich men, weep and howl for your miseries that shall come upon you. Your riches are corrupted, and your garments are moth-eaten. Your gold and silver is cankered; and the rust of them shall be a witness against you, and shall eat your flesh as it were fire. Ye have heaped treasure together for the last days. Behold, the hire of the labourers who have reaped down your fields, which is of you kept back by fraud, crieth: and the cries of them which have reaped are entered into the ears of the Lord of sabaoth. Ye have lived in pleasure on the earth, and been wanton; ye have nourished your hearts, as in a day of slaughter. Ye have condemned and killed the just; and he doth not resist you **(James 5:1-6 KJV).**

When we fail to connect our lives, finances, and resources to the Kingdom of God, we risk experiencing the negative consequences described in James 5: moth-eaten garments, rust corrosion, and theft. However, when we prioritize the Kingdom of God and seek to connect to its anointing, we can experience blessings and preservation that are not subject to these negative forces. By giving, tithing, and making the Kingdom of God a priority, we can bring preservation upon ourselves and all that has been entrusted to us. This highlights the importance of sowing and reaping, particularly when it comes to our relationship with the Kingdom of God.

WHEN YOU SOW, YOU REAP!

The Shunammite woman in 2 Kings 4:8-37 is an example of how connecting your life, business, or ministry to the anointing can bring about blessings and increase. She sowed into the life of Elisha and, as a result, received a prophet's reward, which brought new life in the things that were barren and growth to her situation. In the example of the Shunammite woman, when she connected to the anointing in the prophet Elisha, she conceived a child after being barren; and after several years the child died, but was raised back to life by that same anointing.

What anointing was it? It was the anointing of preservation; because rather than her child be left for dead, his life was preserved by the anointing to which she was connected! This is a powerful illustration of the benefits of connecting to the anointing, not only for business people but for all who seek to grow in their relationship with the Lord and bless others. When we stay connected to the anointing, it can help our businesses from failing, our finances from declining, and our lives from becoming stagnant. I encourage you to commit to connecting to the anointing and stay connected to experience all that God has for you.

Looking further in the story of the Shunammite woman, as I mentioned it teaches us about the power of connecting to and staying connected to the anointing. When she became pregnant after being barren, she experienced new life and growth, and when her son later died as a teenager, she returned to the same anointing and power source and he was raised from the dead. This illustrates the transformative and preserving power of the anointing and how it can bring new life and growth to our lives.

Because it had this kind of impact on the Shunammite woman, how much more can it benefit us if we also seek to connect and stay connected to the anointing? Remember to draw upon this source of power and strength in your own life, and watch as it brings transformation and preservation in all areas.

ANOINTING FOR LIFE

Now let's go to the New Testament, in Mark 5, where Jesus is operating in His anointing to restore a demon-possessed man, raise a dead girl, and heal a sick woman. This chapter is filled with miracles caused by Jesus who was and is the anointing connector. The tormented man connected with Jesus and the legion of demons left him. Then Jesus told the man to *"Go home to your friends, and tell them what great things the Lord has done for you, and how He has had compassion on you"* (Mark 5:19 NKJV). Jesus told the man to spread the anointing to others— by ministering in the power of the Holy Spirit's power.

Also in Mark 5, Jesus demonstrated the transformative power of His anointing when He went with a distraught father to his daughter's bedside. Jesus took the child's hand and, through the power of His anointing, brought her back to life by saying, *"Little girl, I say to you, arise"* (Mark 5:41 NKJV). Immediately, the girl arose and was restored to health and her life was preserved. This miraculous event serves as a testament to the power of Jesus's anointing and its ability to bring life and healing to those in need.

SHARE THE POWER OF GOD'S ANOINTING.

Similarly, in Mark 5, a woman with health problems for many years heard about Jesus and made her way through the crowd to touch His clothes, hoping to connect to His anointing of preservation. As a result, her body was immediately healed. Jesus, aware that power had gone out of Him, turned around in the crowd and asked, *"Who touched My clothes?"* When the woman admitted that it was her, Jesus said to her, *"Daughter, your faith has made you well. Go in peace, and be healed of your affliction"* (Mark 5:25-34 NKJV). This story illustrates the transformative power of Jesus's anointing and how it can bring healing, restoration and again, preservation to those who seek it through faith.

Spreading God's anointing can take many different forms, and you too can share it with others through your anointing from God. If you are concerned about your kids, you can lay your hands on their clothing, schoolbooks, or toothbrush and pray over them for peaceful rest and godly dreams. If your spouse is not saved or is struggling with negative behavior, you can take him or her by the hand, show love through touch and kind words, and pray for transformation through the power of the anointing. Remember that the anointing is a powerful force for good and can bring healing, restoration, and transformation to those around you. Seek to share it with others through your words, actions, and prayers.

When you connect someone to the anointing, it destroys yokes. It frees them to be the person God intended.

In Mark 5, we read about individuals who faced significant challenges. These challenges could be present in various aspects of our lives, such as our health, relationships, or work. As Christians, it is our right to seek preservation and healing through the anointing. If you desire to preserve your marriage, family, health, or business, it is possible through the power of the anointing.

One thing we know for sure is that the *anointing of preservation* protects and preserves the attacks of the enemy when words of faith are spoken. Jesus was protected by this anointing, causing those who tried to arrest Him to fall backward. John the Baptist and Jesus were anointed to confront sin and injustice in the political realm, and we must do the same with love and courage.

In the next chapter, we are going to look at the Spirit of Truth! We will find in the lives of David, Elisha, John the Baptist, and others how to connect to the anointing to bring transformation.

3

THE SPIRIT OF TRUTH

*I will pray the Father, and He will give you another Helper, that He may abide with you forever–the **Spirit of truth**, whom the world cannot receive, because it neither sees Him nor knows Him; but you know Him, for He dwells with you and will be in you* (John 14:16-17 NKJV).

I t is essential to connect with the anointing of God, as it carries the Spirit of truth from the Holy Spirit. This is why it is important to be discerning and avoid false anointings that are spread by the devil. This is why we are told by Jesus to beware of "false christs" in the day we live in (Matthew 24:24). In other words, these are things that look anointed or carry a false anointing thus becoming a false christ. These false anointings do not come from the Holy Spirit, but rather from the devil, the father of lies.

It is crucial to be mindful of what and whom you connect with. If you constantly expose yourself to negative influences, such as destructive social media, false news, and harmful media coverage, you may absorb negative anointing that brings with it feelings of anxiety, fear, worry, stress, and tension. On the other hand, God's anointing brings with it His truth, joy, love, and peace.

By connecting with God's anointing and walking in it, you can destroy negativity, fear, deception, and anything else the enemy may try to use to control your life. It is important to protect the anointing that not only preserves your life but also your peace.

In the conversation between Elijah and Elisha in 2 Kings 2:9 (NKJV), Elisha asks for a double portion of Elijah's spirit.

> *And so it was, when they had crossed over, that Elijah said to Elisha, "Ask! What may I do for you, before I am taken away from you?" Elisha said, "Please let a double portion of your spirit be upon me."*

This request may seem strange at first glance, but it highlights the importance of the anointing and its ability to bring preservation to one's life. By asking for a double portion of Elijah's spirit, Elisha is seeking to connect with the anointing that Elijah possessed and to receive the benefits and protections that come with it. This passage serves as a reminder of the value of the anointing and the importance of seeking it in our own lives.

Elisha knew the value of the anointing and recognized it when he saw it. We must also strive to understand what the anointing is and isn't. This is why, after undergoing several tests with his mentor Elijah in Bethel, Gilgal, Jericho, and Jordan, Elisha refused to leave Elijah's side. He knew that by staying connected to the anointing that was upon

Elijah, he would be able to benefit from its protection and power. (See 2 Kings 2.)

The tests that Elisha underwent in Bethel, Gilgal, Jericho, and Jordan were crucial in helping him to receive the double portion of the anointing that rested upon Elijah and to preserve that anointing in his own life. These tests, starting with the test of Bethel, which means the House of God, demonstrated the importance of connecting to the House of God, an anointed pastor, and the body of Christ to receive preservation. This is as we learned in the previous chapter in Mark 5 about the woman with the issue of blood. She had many "issues" for twelve years that offered her no help and drained her resources. Sounds like today, for some? Yet, when she connected to the anointing found in Jesus's garment or the "body of Christ," all her issues stopped. This was because the body of Christ, or the body of believers, the local church is to carry the anointing that helps others by destroying yokes and undoing heavy burdens—resulting in preservation over their lives.

We see in addition, Ephesians 4.11 states, the fivefold ministry brings this preservation to believers by equipping them for the work of the ministry and protecting them from being swayed by false doctrine or other distractions that may hinder their walk with the Lord. It is essential to pass these tests and stay connected to the anointing to experience its full benefits and protection for yourself.

The next test that Elisha faced on his journey to receive the double portion of Elijah's anointing was at Gilgal, the place where the Israelites stopped receiving manna from Heaven and had to start gathering their food. This test is significant in terms of the anointing of preservation because it highlights the importance of connecting to the Word of God and pursuing a disciplined, committed life of seeking the Kingdom of God.

To preserve the anointing in our lives, we must be willing to put in the work and focus on spiritual matters, rather than relying on external factors or indulging in carnal, compromising, or worldly pursuits. It requires discipline and a dedication to God to maintain the anointing and all that it brings. This is why God gave the children of Israel manna in the morning and quail or flesh at night!

> *...At even ye shall eat flesh, and in the morning ye shall be filled with bread; and ye shall know that I am the Lord your God. And it came to pass, that at even the quails came up, and covered the camp: and in the morning the dew lay round about the host* **(Exodus 16:12-13 KJV)**.

How profound is this prophetic prototype of how we can activate and increase the anointing that preserves over our lives and family. It comes by manna in the morning, starting with God, His Word and carrying His presence throughout the day. Then the rest of day can be quail, not as in walking in the flesh but enjoying our life here on earth knowing we are covered in His anointing because we prioritized Him first.

The next stop for Elisha was Jericho. As we know from the story in the Bible, Jericho was a heavily fortified city that the Israelites conquered by marching around its walls and shouting on the seventh lap, causing the walls to collapse. God supernaturally flattened these walls! This event demonstrates the power of the anointing to bring victory in spiritual warfare and to provide preservation for those who trust in God. Just like Rahab and her family in Jericho were spared when they hung a scarlet thread from their window to signal their allegiance to the Israelites, we can also experience preservation when we stand firm in our faith and do not tolerate the enemy's schemes and attacks.

The anointing is also for battle, as exemplified by David's defeat of Goliath. It was not just the rock that David used in his sling that took down the giant, but the anointing on the rock that brought victory and preservation for David and all of Israel. In the same way, you too are anointed for victory, and as you press through the battles that come your way, you will be victorious and preserved from the hand of the enemy.

Finally, Elisha faced the last test that relates to preserving the anointing in our lives: the test of Jordan. This test took place at a time of transition and crossing over. It is important to remember that the anointing is for action, not for staying stagnant. Elisha had the choice to stay on the other side of the Jordan with the 50 sons of the prophets, who were merely spectators, or to make the transition into deeper commitment and come out of old ways. By crossing over the Jordan and receiving the double portion of Elijah's mantle, Elisha was able to preserve his life and ministry. This test illustrates the importance of acting and moving forward in our faith to preserve the anointing in our lives.

Elisha understood the importance of connecting to the anointing and was willing to go through the necessary steps, as represented by Bethel, Gilgal, Jericho, and Jordan, rather than miss out on its benefits. Unfortunately, many people today are content to take the easy or compromised route and do not prioritize preserving the anointing in their lives. However, the anointing of preservation is not only available, it is also subject to our daily decisions and lifestyles. Just as Elisha chose to connect with what would ultimately preserve his life and ministry, we must be wise in what we connect to and pay attention to the spirit behind what is being said. This will help us to stay on track and receive the full benefits of the anointing.

Jesus tells us:

> **Take heed that no one deceives you**. For many will come in My name, saying, "I am the Christ," and will deceive many. And you will hear of wars and rumors of wars. See that you are not troubled; for all these things must come to pass, but the end is not yet. ...Then many false prophets will rise up and deceive many. ...Then if anyone says to you, "Look, here is the Christ!" or "There!" do not believe it. For false christs and false prophets will rise and show great signs and wonders to deceive, if possible, even the elect. See, I have told you beforehand (Matthew 24:4-6,11,23-25 NKJV).

It is important to remember Jesus's warning as was mentioned about false christs or false anointings, and not allow us to be deceived. Jesus mentioned this three times, emphasizing the importance of being on guard against these false anointings. Remember, "Christ" means anointed, and "Christian" means anointed one, so it is easy to see how people might be misled by those who appear to be anointed but are not.

The rise of the "woke culture" in some churches is one example of this, as some preachers try to be trendy and relevant at the expense of biblical truth, to avoid offending anyone. However, this is not the way to connect with the anointing that destroys yokes and undoes heavy burdens. Instead, it is likely to lead to a connection with demonic spirits that burden and deceive a generation. It is crucial to be discerning and to avoid false anointings to stay on the right path.

As Jesus warned, there will be many "false christs" and false anointings in the world, so it is important to connect with the righteous, godly anointing if we want to advance God's Kingdom on earth. One way to distinguish between true and false anointings is to examine whether they align with Scripture and Kingdom principles as taught by Jesus. If an anointing promotes worldliness, carnality, or compromise, it is likely not from God and should be avoided. On the other hand, a righteous, godly anointing will line up with the teachings of Scripture and help us to live by Kingdom principles. By being discerning and seeking the true anointing, we can better serve God and His Kingdom.

To summarize, living in and declaring God's anointing as a lifestyle, and spending time reading the Word of God, can help us to recognize when someone is speaking something that is not in line with the truth of God's anointing. When we are immersed in the anointing and seek to follow it in our daily lives, we are better equipped to discern the truth and avoid false teachings.

THE TRUTH IS FOUND IN GOD'S WORD.

When people, especially pastors, are more concerned with being accepted by the culture and being trendy and relevant than with upholding their authority and the anointing of God, they risk losing their anointing. This is because they are prioritizing the values of the culture over the values of the Kingdom of God and aligning themselves more with the spirit of the culture than with the Spirit of God. It is important to remember that the anointing comes from God and should not be compromised to conform to the world.

It's no wonder John the Baptist was such a quirky guy, with his camel hair clothes and locust-filled diet (Matthew 3:4). He was determined and marked by God to stand out from the crowd and deliver his exciting message: Jesus, the Son of God, was right there with them, ready to be baptized. John knew he couldn't let the culture's demands for relevancy interfere with his anointing, so he stayed connected to it and called people to repentance, preparing the way for the Messiah's ministry, which would be empowered by the same anointing. John was determined not to compromise, be complacent, or connect to the wrong things, as he had to protect the holy anointing to experience its full manifestation and preservation. Talk about dedication!

CHOOSE WISELY

As we learned from Elisha, it is important to be mindful of what and whom we associate with, as this can have a significant impact on our lives. Elisha recognized the value of the anointing that Elijah had and desired a double portion of it for himself. We should also desire to tap into God's anointing to lead a full and fulfilled life. Choosing our friends and associates wisely can help us to "drip with the anointing," as the people we surround ourselves with can influence and shape our lives. It is important to be intentional about these relationships and to make sure that we are aligning ourselves with those who will help us to grow and thrive in our faith.

DRIP OVER PEOPLE WITH GOD'S ANOINTING.

Elisha knew a good thing when he saw it—he recognized that Elijah was a man of God who was overflowing with divine favor. He probably thought to himself, *I'm sticking to this guy like glue! If I hang around him, maybe some of that awesome anointing will rub off on me.* And that's why you should never settle for a lifeless church—you want to be part of a thriving, anointed community where the Holy Spirit is present and active.

> *So **Elijah went and found Elisha** son of Shaphat plowing a field. There were twelve teams of oxen in the field, and Elisha was plowing with the twelfth team. **Elijah went over to him and threw his cloak across his shoulders** and then walked away. **Elisha left the oxen standing there, ran after Elijah,** and said to him, "First let me go and kiss my father and mother good-bye, and then I will go with you!" Elijah replied, "Go on back, but think about what I have done to you." So Elisha returned to his oxen and slaughtered them. He used the wood from the plow to build a fire to roast their flesh. He passed around the meat to the townspeople, and they all ate. **Then he went with Elijah as his assistant** (1 Kings 19:19-21 NLT).*

TASTE THE ANOINTING

Second, you must get a taste of the anointing. As 1 Kings 19:19 says, *"Elijah went to Elisha and threw his cloak across his shoulders."* This passage tells us that Elijah, the great prophet, bestowed upon Elisha the gift of his anointed mantle. Elisha, feeling something he had never felt before, left his oxen behind and ran after Elijah. He even said, *"First let me go and kiss my father and mother, goodbye, and then I will go with you!"*

In other words, Elisha was acknowledging the profound impact of the anointing and wanted to pay his respects before fully committing to this new path. And that's a lesson for all of us—when we receive the anointing, it may require us to say goodbye to certain things we love. But trust me, it's worth it. Once you get a taste of the anointing, your life will change for the better.

I am hungry for God and His anointing! I crave His presence with every fiber of my being. I don't care what anyone else thinks—I only care about what God thinks of me. I love Him deeply, and I know He knows I do. When you experience the transformative power of God's anointing, you never want to go back to life without it. That's why I steer clear of books that might offer some temporal comfort but do nothing to nourish my spirit. No, I want the real deal—I want the fire of the anointing always burning within me!

FEED YOUR SPIRIT WITH GOD'S TRUTH.

As a man of God, it's my mission to soak up godly, righteous, and anointed truths. That's why I stay away from the negativity of the news—I don't want any of that toxic energy inside me. When you taste the anointing, it will grow and flourish within you. It's something that can be measured, increased, or decreased. Jesus had the anointing without measure, but our anointing can be influenced by the people and places we associate with.

I have tried to work hard to pass the necessary tests and pay the price for a strong anointing. And let me tell you, it was worth it. I've faced my fair share of trials and challenges, but through it all, God has guided me. He told me to stay at Gilgal, Bethel, and Jericho, and I have done my best to obey. Every test I faced was an opportunity to learn and grow in my faith. You must love His anointing. It's the presence of God!

Elisha understood that accepting the anointing came at a price. He said to Elijah, "Let me just say goodbye to my mom and dad before I go." He knew that he might not see his family again for a long time, if ever. This is the reality for those who are chosen by God—we must be willing to pay the price, no matter what it may be. The anointing comes with its own set of challenges and sacrifices, but the reward of being used by God to do His work is immeasurable.

This determined focus and hunger for the anointing is also what made the Philistines realize there was something supernatural about the Ark of the Covenant (1 Samuel 6). What was it about this golden box that was supposed to carry the power of God? They discovered this after putting the ark upon the backs of two momma cows, and sending it back to Israel after it caused the Philistines quite a lot of discomfort. It was the fact the momma cows never turned around to the cries of their young calves because of the anointing that was upon their shoulders. In the same way, it is not that we don't serve our household respectfully first, but rather meaning when the anointing is upon us we are to carry it with focus, honor, reverence, and dedication with the assignments given to us by the Lord.

THE PRESENCE OF GOD IS FOUND IN HIS ANOINTING.

So how do we receive the anointing of preservation? The laying on of hands is indeed one way to transmit the anointing, but it's not the only way. The anointing can also be released through words—when you speak God's Word, when you speak the anointed word, things begin to move. Jesus knew this well—when He started His ministry, He declared, *"The Spirit of the Lord God is upon Me, because He has anointed Me..."* (Luke 4:18 NKJV). These are powerful, anointed words that can unleash God's goodness in your life. So don't be afraid to speak them out loud—you never know what kind of transformation they might bring.

This is the first thing Jesus did as He started His ministry. He declared His anointing.

DECLARE YOUR ANOINTING

Do you feel like you have a special purpose in life? If you answered yes, then the first thing you need to do is embrace the fact that you are anointed. Are you called to run for office in your community, state, or even on the national level? Then you need to declare, "The Spirit of the Lord is upon me and I'm anointed! I'm anointed! The Spirit of the Lord is on me for this calling!" If you're a teacher who feels called to spread the love of God in your school, then you need to say, "I'm anointed! The Spirit of the Lord is on me to represent Him in my local education system!" And once you recognize your own anointing, it's important to surround yourself with other people who are anointed as well. Together, you can encourage and motivate each other to fulfill your calling with boldness and confidence.

Jesus knew exactly who He was and what He was called to do. He was reading from the book of Isaiah and declared that He was anointed to *"preach the gospel to the poor; ...to heal the brokenhearted, to proclaim liberty to the captives and recovery of sight to the blind, to set at liberty those who are oppressed; to proclaim the acceptable year of the Lord"* (Luke 4:18-19 NKJV). And the power of His anointing was present in His words. As believers, we too have been anointed and our words carry the weight of that anointing. Let us use them wisely and with purpose.

The anointing is on our words. After Jesus declared in Luke 4:21 (NLT), *"The Scripture you've just heard has been fulfilled this very day!"* the people were confused knowing that Jesus was Joseph the carpenter's son. So then Jesus said:

> *"You will undoubtedly quote me this proverb: 'Physician, heal yourself'—meaning, 'Do miracles here in your hometown like those you did in Capernaum.' But I tell you the truth, no prophet is accepted in his own hometown. Certainly there were many needy widows in Israel in Elijah's time, when the heavens were closed for three and a half years, and a severe famine devastated the land. Yet Elijah was not sent to any of them. He was sent instead to a foreigner—a widow of Zarephath in the land of Sidon. And many in Israel had leprosy in the time of the prophet Elisha, but the only one healed was Naaman, a Syrian." When they heard this, the people in the synagogue were furious. Jumping up, they mobbed him and forced him to the edge of the hill on which the town was built. They intended to push him over the cliff, but he passed right through the crowd and went on his way* (**Luke 4:23-30 NLT**).

Jesus knew that not everyone would accept His message and many of His people would reject Him. When He shared this truth at the synagogue, the people became so enraged that they wanted to throw Him off a cliff and kill Him. But Jesus was able to pass through the angry crowd unscathed. How did He do it? He relied on the power of the anointing of preservation to protect Him. By declaring His connection to this divine favor, Jesus was able to walk away from a potentially dangerous situation without harm.

He declared that *"The Spirit of the Lord is upon Me,"* so they couldn't touch Him. They could do Him no harm—until the proper time when Jesus sacrificially allowed them to crucify Him. When you are anointed, you are preserved! No weapon formed against you will prosper. You have the authority to condemn any tongue that rises against you in judgment because you are anointed.

They couldn't take Jesus's life because of the powerful proclamation coming out of His mouth that activated the anointing of preservation. And as a result, He was able to walk right through that angry mob unscathed. Embrace the anointing on your life and know that you are protected and preserved by the power of God.

TAPPING INTO THE ANOINTING WITHIN

Why is it so important to understand the power of anointed language, especially speaking in tongues? Because when you pray in this way, you are activating the anointing with your words. This is what sets the Old Testament and the New Testament apart. There were certainly anointed prophecies and miraculous signs and wonders in the Old Testament, but they didn't have the gift of anointed, supernatural language known as speaking in tongues. This elevates the anointing to a whole new level. In the Old Testament, the anointing came upon people from the outside; in the New Testament, through the indwelling of the Holy Spirit, the anointing comes from within us. This is a game-changer for believers.

PROCLAIM JESUS AS LORD

By declaring, as Jesus did, that the Spirit of the Lord is upon you, you too can escape the enemy. When you pray in tongues, it has the power to make a real difference in your life. In John 7:38 (NIV), Jesus says, *"Whoever believes in me, as Scripture has said, rivers of living water will flow from within them."* How could Jesus be speaking about the Spirit, about the anointing that resides within us, when the Holy Spirit had not yet been given? The answer is that Jesus was teaching us that when we are filled with the Holy Spirit, anointed words will flow from within us.

Every time you speak or pray in tongues, you tap into the river of life that flows from the anointing within you, which comes through the baptism of the Holy Spirit. And in the same way, when you speak or pray anointed words, you activate that anointing and allow it to work in your life. It's a powerful, transformative experience that can change the course of your life for the better.

OLD TESTAMENT TRUTH AND NEW TESTAMENT APPLICATION

Now, let's delve into the Old Testament to find historical proof and truths that apply to our lives in the New Testament. The Bible is not just a work of fiction—it's literal, living, and as alive today as it was when it was first written. The truths contained within it are timeless and applicable to every person at every point in history. Consider the story of Noah and the Flood. Most people know that it was a real event that happened, but what does it mean for us today? Keeping in mind Jesus's words about *"rivers of living water"* in John 7:38, let's look at this passage in Genesis:

> *When Noah was 600 years old, on the seventeenth day of the second month, all the underground waters erupted from the earth, and the rain fell in mighty torrents from the sky* (Genesis 7:11 NLT).

In other words, the earth literally burst open. But how does this apply prophetically? John 7:38 tells us that out of our hearts, our inner selves will flow rivers of living water. Could this be a metaphor for the outpouring of the Holy Spirit in our lives? It's certainly worth considering.

Psalm 42:7 (NKJV) says, *"Deep calls unto deep at the noise of Your waterfalls...."* Where is this "deep" located? In your spirit. This is why the King James translation of John 7:38 says that the flow of the Spirit as living water, would come from deep within our bellies, speaking of our spirits. When you start praying in tongues, you put some serious power behind your prayers. You tap into the anointing within you and release it. You open up the fountain of your deep. You're doing exactly what is described in Genesis 7:11 (NKJV) when it says, *"the fountains of the great deep were broken up, and the windows of heaven were opened."* Whatever comes out of you activates the supernatural. The anointing within you is a powerful force, and when you pray in tongues, you unleash it in a powerful way. This is key for walking in and activating the supernatural power of God.

YOU CAN ACTIVATE THE SUPERNATURAL.

We must learn to press deeper and learn how to pray in tongues with a fervency and release the floodgates of the anointing within you. When you do you, it helps you to receive the living water that will satisfy your thirst for eternity. In Genesis 7:11, the fountains of the deep were opened up; and in John 7, Jesus tells us that this is a prophetic application for us. This is why we need to tap into what's inside us and unleash anointed words through prayer in tongues. It's an exciting way to connect with God and access the power and strength that comes from His anointing. Don't miss out on this incredible opportunity to experience His presence in a deeper way.

If you are hungry and thirst for more, we must do what Jesus said to the woman at the well in John chapter 4. He said, *"Come and drink."* This speaks not only of salvation that satisfies every longing and thirst, but it also positions us then for the greater depths in God that comes with being filled with the Holy Spirit and power! It is the powerful river of life that flows out of you, changing you and empowering you to minister to others. If you are thirsting for more of Him and want that living water of salvation or perhaps you have and want to be filled with the Holy Spirit, I have provided an opportunity for you to do just that at the end of this book in the final chapter.

Now that we have discovered the need for the rivers of living water that flow when we pray in tongues, what about the anointing of preservation, and how does this example further apply to our lives? In Genesis 7:11, we see that the earth broke open, waters poured out from beneath, and came down from above. Did God allow all life to be washed away and drowned? No, He preserved Noah and his family, as well as males and females of every species, by providing a way for them to enter the ark and be saved.

Noah was not preserved just by his own might or power but something that was protecting, preserving his life and family. It was God Himself, through His wonderful Spirit. This is a powerful example of the anointing of preservation at work, protecting and preserving those who trust in God and follow His instructions. The anointing of preservation is a powerful force that can help us navigate through difficult times and come out unscathed just like with Noah and those in the ark.

> Then **the Lord said to Noah, "Come into the ark, you and all your household, because I have seen that you are righteous before Me** in this generation. *You shall take with you seven each of every clean animal, a male and his female; two each of animals that are unclean, a male and his female; also seven each of birds of the air, male and female, to keep the species alive on the face of all the earth. For after seven more days I will cause it to rain on the earth forty days and forty nights, and I will destroy from the face of the earth all living things that I have made." And Noah did according to all that the Lord commanded him. ...And they went into the ark to Noah, two by two, of all flesh in which is the breath of life.* **So those that entered, male and female of all flesh, went in as God had commanded him; and the Lord shut him in** (Genesis 7:1-5,15-16 NKJV).

So what happened? The Lord shut Noah in the ark and preserved him. This is once again a beautiful prophetic example of the day of Pentecost when Jesus told the disciples and those in the upper room to tarry and shut themselves up until they receive power from on high.

> *And, behold, I send the promise of my Father upon you: but tarry ye in the city of Jerusalem,*

until ye be endued with power from on high (Luke 24:49 KJV).

Now this is not to imply we must wait for the Holy Spirit's infilling, if that's the case then we would need to go to Jerusalem per the instruction of Jesus. So, then what is the prophetic application for us today? When we shut ourselves in by spending time with the Lord, praying in tongues, we activate the Holy Spirit within us, and preservation is the result. The message here is clear: pray in tongues and speak in tongues often, and you'll release the anointing from your spirit to bring preservation into your life. It is key to getting the river of power flowing and even activating the gifts of God with in you, not only preserving you but what we have been entrusted by the Lord.

This happened in Acts 10 at the house of Cornelius when they were filled with the Holy Spirit, they began to prophesy as gifts were activated in them. Imagine what happens in your life as you pray in the spirit and the gifts are activated; but more than that, you are releasing divine preservation over yourself and what you are praying for!

We encounter a fresh anointing when we pray in the Holy Spirit as mentioned in Acts 2:4 (NKJV): *"They were all filled with the Holy Spirit and began to speak with other tongues, as the Spirit gave them utterance."* Not only does this anointing come upon us but it resides within us, enabling us to discern spiritual matters such as stated by 1 Corinthians 2:13 (NKJV): *"These things we also speak, not in words which man's wisdom teaches but which the Holy Spirit teaches, comparing spiritual things with spiritual."*

By praying in unknown tongues, we awaken the river of God's power that flows through us. The Bible says you don't always know how to pray as you want, but the Spirit with anointed language, and anointed words, prays through you and out of you and for you—and part of that is God's version of anointed preservation.

ACTIVATE THE RIVER FLOW OVER YOUR LIFE.

Strengthening our relationship with God and staying devoted to Him is not only beneficial for ourselves but also protects His divine will. Jude 1:20-21 (NKJV) advises us, *"...building yourselves up on your most holy faith, praying in the Holy Spirit, keep yourselves in the love of God, looking for the mercy of our Lord Jesus Christ unto eternal life."* Through prayer in the Holy Spirit we can create a protective shield around us and those around us; therefore, securing the fulfillment of His promises.

This chapter has emphasized the importance of praying in tongues and speaking in tongues to tap into the anointing within us and release it in our lives. By doing so, we can experience the anointing of preservation, protecting, and preserving us in difficult times. It's a powerful way to connect with God and access His strength and power in our lives.

Are you ready to go another level in the anointing? In the next chapter, we will uncover ways to boost and safeguard the anointing of preservation in our lives. You won't want to miss these important truths—get ready to learn some powerful strategies for accessing and maintaining this important anointing.

4

INCREASING GOD'S ANOINTING

*Therefore, as through one man's [Adam] offense judgment came to all men, resulting in condemnation, even so **through one Man's [Jesus] righteous act the free gift came to all** men, resulting in justification of life* (Romans 5:18 NKJV).

Isaiah 10:27 teaches us that God's anointing is when He shows up in human flesh to do what no human could ever accomplish—something supernatural, something extraordinary! That's the power of the anointing. Let's explore how to maximize the anointing of God that has been bestowed upon you. It's time to take a deeper dive into growing the power of His divine touch in your life!

YOUR COVENANT WITH GOD

I've come to understand that the anointing of God is preserved in three key powerful ways: 1) our covenant with Him; 2) His Word; as well as 3) fellowshipping and knowing the Holy Spirit. Through these, we can tap into the miraculous power of His divine touch!

Romans 10:9-10 (NKJV) tells us:

> *if you confess with your mouth the Lord Jesus and believe in your heart that God has raised Him from the dead, you will be saved. For with the heart one believes unto righteousness, and with the mouth confession is made unto salvation.*

When we confess, we are saved and we enter into a powerful covenant with God through the blood of Jesus Christ. This is not just a promise of forgiveness of sin and eternal life, it's even greater than that! We sometimes only see the promise of Heaven and think that salvation is limited to this. But there is much more to being "saved" than just being forgiven and living out eternity in Heaven!

According to our opening Scripture about Jesus's *"free gift,"* God gives us eternal life in Christ and a righteous life even while we live on this earth. As the apostle Paul wrote in Romans 10:13, *"For whoever calls on the name of the Lord shall be saved."* The word *sozo* (Greek word for "save") means forgiveness of sins, which also means healing of your body. This healing has already been provided; it's already been accomplished! Believe it; you're already healed!

YOUR COVENANT INCLUDES HEALTH AND PROSPERITY/BLESSING.

Your physical healing and long life is part of your free-gift package. Thank You, Jesus, for willingly giving up Your life at the young age of 33 so that we may live a long life and fulfill our God-given purpose. He became the curse so that premature death would not befall us. When people witness someone pass away prematurely, they might think it is inevitable; however, our *sozo* rights package has provided preservation and even long life! It has already been provided in the fulfilled, ratified blood of our covenant.

This is why we need to speak this covenant blessing over us and loved ones, releasing the anointing of preservation that preserves us for a healthy long life. We are to be satisfied with long life according to Psalm 91:16. There is no satisfaction to a life cut short prematurely. How about the promise of long life God gave to Abraham that is ours through the same covenant right given him? The Lord entered covenant with him, and the benefit given was Abraham would go to his fathers in peace, not premature death, sickness, tragedy, and calamity. Look at this covenant promise.

And thou shalt go to thy fathers in peace; thou shalt be buried in a good old age (Genesis 15:15 KJV).

All who come to God through Jesus have the same covenant right to this as Abraham. How is that you may ask? We find this linking of the covenant of Abraham to us and all its benefits through Jesus Christ in what is revealed in Galatians 3:13-14 (KJV):

> *Christ hath redeemed us from the curse of the law, being made a curse for us: for it is written, Cursed is every one that hangeth on a tree: That the blessing of Abraham might come on the Gentiles through Jesus Christ; that we might receive the promise of the Spirit through faith.*

Notice that covenant and its benefits are now ours because of Jesus. This means we have the right to claim health, and the same long life given to Abraham through covenant with God. We can go to our fathers in peace, meaning nothing missing, nothing broken and not be held in the jaws of sickness and disease. This is why understanding our covenant in relation to the anointing of preservation is vital. It will actually help to prolong our lives and better them when we know what is rightfully ours. We not only have the promise of peace but also when we depart this earth it will be in a good old age.

Perhaps this is why David said to the Lord, to teach us to number our days. I believe this means that we aren't to let others speak death, tragedy, or calamity over us, nor should we do the same. We may not be one who uses profanity, but we have to be careful we don't curse. What I mean is, that we don't curse our own lives or others by speaking negativity, sickness, or death. We have a covenant right and an anointing that preserves us for an abundant life that Jesus promised we could have.

We furthermore have been redeemed; our lives, health, and well-being have been paid for by Jesus Christ when He shed His precious blood. It literally paid for our lives to be preserved from the onslaughts of the enemy, and things that come to steal, kill, and even destroy like sickness, disease, tragedies, and calamities. Look at what David described as part of our preservation covenant package given to us through Jesus.

> *Bless the Lord, O my soul, and forget not all his benefits* **(Psalm 103:2 KJV).**

I want you to see something that is part of this benefits package. It is the fact that we have been redeemed from destruction.

> *Who redeemeth thy life from destruction; who crowneth thee with lovingkindness and tender mercies* **(Psalm 103:4 KJV).**

This means sickness, premature death, tragedy, and calamities certainly are what we are redeemed from.

We must always remember that health, long life, and blessings are part of the gospel and free gift of salvation. This is because, in addition to forgiveness of sin, your free-gift package comes with so much more, including healing, wholeness, soundness of mind, a blessed memory, rescue from any form of harm or danger, and protection as well as preservation. It is all part of the anointing of preservation you receive when you call on the name of the Lord and are saved. Therefore, good health and wealth also form part of this special free-gift package.

THE ANOINTING MEANS PROTECTION.

Thanks to the anointing of preservation, we can be protected, just as Jesus was. According to Acts 10:37-38, it is clear that God anointed Jesus with the Holy Spirit and power. This was further confirmed—as has been mentioned and as we have come to understand—when He read from Isaiah in the synagogue, proclaiming, *"The Spirit of the Lord is upon Me, because He has anointed Me... Today this Scripture is fulfilled in your hearing"* (Luke 4:18-21 NKJV). To access this same protection and anointing in our lives, we need to call upon the name of the Lord. When we do, we are saved, not just in eternal life but also granted a full benefits covenant package that brings preservation to save and protect.

GOD PRESERVES THROUGH HIS WORD

In the same way as Noah, the Bible tells us that no evil could touch Jesus, and we can experience the same protection if we call on His name as well. Despite being the Son of God, Jesus, as pointed out before, experienced many attempted attacks before His ultimate sacrifice in Golgotha. These included attempts from King Herod, who tried to have Jesus killed while He was still an infant (Matthew 2:13-18); the Pharisees and scribes who wanted to trap Him with their questions (Luke 11:53-54); and the Jewish leaders and Roman soldiers who sought to arrest Him at Gethsemane (Luke 22:47-48). No matter how hard they tried, none of these attempts were successful—evil never won against Jesus—and it won't against us either.

Jesus proclaimed that no enemy could end His life until He gave permission. As evidenced in John 7, many people were out for His blood but He evaded them every time. It was through this sacrificial death that Jesus took upon the curse and became the sin offering and sacrifice for the sake of all mankind so that we can be blessed.

Think for a moment when Jesus was baptized by John the Baptist and how something significant took place in His life:

> *When all the people were baptized, it came to pass that Jesus also was baptized; and while He prayed, the heaven was opened. And **the Holy Spirit descended in bodily form like a dove upon Him**, and a voice came from heaven which*

said, "You are My beloved Son; in You I am well pleased" (Luke 3:21-22 NKJV).

The Bible says that the Spirit of God came upon Jesus and God the Father was well pleased.

Immediately after Jesus was baptized and filled with the Holy Spirit:

> *Then **Jesus, being filled with the Holy Spirit**, returned from the Jordan and **was led by the Spirit into the wilderness**, being tempted for forty days by the devil...* (Luke 4:1-2 NKJV).

God's Spirit led Jesus into a battle of the ages, to confront the devil, full of the Holy Spirit and make a stand for the Kingdom of God. Today, we may be facing battles or a huge conflict in our nation, but through the Holy Spirit and the power of His Word we prevail. I want you to be encouraged, because you may feel your efforts or any efforts to see our nation turn around are fruitless because of the intensity of the battle.

Yet we must always remember, whether it be concerning our lives, our loved ones, our cities or our nation, conflict is only meant to energize God's anointing! This will always produce powerful results that will vanquish any enemy attacking us or our nation. Our adversary has overreached himself this time; but instead of destroying us, we will be energized by God's power and witness unprecedented blessings as we reclaim souls for Jesus Christ! This is especially true concerning the anointing of preservation that safeguards the United States as it remains intact, promising an abundant harvest of souls ready to follow Him.

KNOWING HIS WORD IS VITAL

We must, like Jesus, continue to speak God's Word in every situation and press deeper into the things of the Spirit. Remember, when Jesus ventured into the wilderness, He faced many temptations from the devil. But Jesus stood firm with God's Word and soundly defeated the wicked one on each occasion. His triumph serves as a reminder to us all the importance of surrendering to our Lord's will!

> *And the devil said to Him, "If You are the Son of God, command this stone to become bread." But Jesus answered him, saying, "**It is written,** 'Man shall not live by bread alone, but by every word of God'"* (Luke 4:3-4 NKJV).

> *"If You will worship before me, all will be Yours." And Jesus answered and said to him, "Get behind Me, Satan! For **it is written**, 'You shall worship the Lord your God, and Him only you shall serve'"* (Luke 4:7-8 NKJV).

> *"If You are the Son of God, throw Yourself down from here. For it is written: 'He shall give His angels charge over you, to keep you,' and, 'In their hands they shall bear you up, lest you dash*

*your foot against a stone.'" And Jesus answered and said to him, "**It has been said**, 'You shall not tempt the Lord your God'"* (Luke 4:9-12 NKJV).

As you can see with the temptation of our Lord in the wilderness. Jesus's anointing and knowledge of God's Word gave Him the power to overcome every temptation from the evil one, preserving His life and calling. His victory spread throughout Galilee, with many coming to witness His teachings in the synagogues and glorifying Him for it (Luke 4:14-15 NKJV). He clearly showed us that we can have the same victorious results, so that we can take courage knowing that nothing can stand against those who have been anointed by our Lord. Jesus came out of the wilderness in the power of the Spirit, and we will come out empowered by the Spirit in every situation as well!

DECLARING HIS WORD IS CRUCIAL.

The anointing is activated as we have seen by our words but also by speaking, knowing the anointed Word of God! When Jesus read from the book of Isaiah and declared His anointing, He activated and increased a powerful force of protection, or preservation, over Himself until it was time for His life to be given in sacrifice. This is why I continue to remind you that in the same way, when you boldly proclaim God's word and declare, "The Spirit of the Lord is upon me! I am anointed," you will experience more security and safety for yourself and your loved ones.

DECLARE YOUR ANOINTING

The time has come for Aaron to join his ancestors in death. He will not enter the land I am giving the people of Israel, because the two of you rebelled against my instructions.... Now take Aaron and his son Eleazar up Mount Hor. There you will remove Aaron's priestly garments and put them on Eleazar, his son. Aaron will die there and join his ancestors." ...At the summit, Moses removed the priestly garments from Aaron and put them on Eleazar, Aaron's son. Then Aaron died there on top of the mountain... (**Numbers 20:24-28 NLT**).

We not only need to declare that we are anointed but protect that precious anointing upon our lives. This is clearly shown when God told Aaron to remove his priestly garments, he died instantly. But as long as he was under the protection of God's anointing, he lived under the preservation it provided.

In the same way, Elijah was preserved from all the attempts on his life by the wicked queen Jezebel. He too, like Aaron, was to give up his garment or mantle; once he did, he was carried into Heaven by the Lord's chariot. This caused his mantle of anointing to be passed on to Elisha. Resulting in the anointing that was still in the mantle of Elijah and was the key to preserving Elisha's life as well. This anointing was so powerful that it brought preservation when others would connect to it, as seen with a widow struggling with debt.

As a group of prophets watched in awe, Elisha provided oil for many empty jars that took care of her burden and kept her and her family safe, preserving them. Sadly, it's evident that these other prophets did not receive the double portion blessed upon the widow through Elisha. Even after the prophet Elisha's passing, we still see the anointing of preservation alive and available to those who would receive it! Think about that for a moment—how powerful the anointing of preservation is and that fact that it still in the bones of a dead man who was anointed! Second Kings 13:21 (NIV) tells us that Elisha's bones were still anointed with preservation in death, we can see how powerful this blessing is.

> *Once while some Israelites were burying a man, suddenly they saw a band of raiders; so they threw the man's body into Elisha's tomb. When the body touched Elisha's bones, the man came to life and stood up on his feet* **(2 Kings 13:21 NIV).**

Think for a moment as in the examples with Aaron, Elijah, and Elisha, the power that was in the anointing they carried. In the same way when Jesus hung on the Cross, His garments were taken from Him by the soldiers. What they didn't realize is the anointing of preservation that was upon the Lord—that even His garments dripped with that precious power! This was evident, especially in how many were supernaturally touched and healed as they touched them. These soldiers were spiritually blinded to the anointing in those garments, that they only saw the monetary value rather than a spiritual benefit or value available for them. They began gambling for them because of the value they brought, being a seamless gown (Luke 23:34). They ignorantly and maliciously stripped Him of His covering and protection.

Yet it also was a symbol, as with the others we discussed, that once the garment was removed, so was the anointing that preserved them. However, the good news is though it was sinful humanity that removed Jesus's mantle, He willingly took on our sin to preserve us all (2 Corinthians 5:21) and soon after poured out His Spirit to empower us with the anointing, preserving our very lives!

Always remember, Jesus's sacrifice was of His choosing. Yet, we reaped the benefits that preserve our lives and families. He told the crowd:

I am the good shepherd; I know my sheep and my sheep know me—just as the Father knows me and I know the Father—and I lay down my life for the sheep. I have other sheep that are not of this sheep pen. I must bring them also. They too will listen to my voice, and there shall be one flock and one shepherd. **The reason my Father loves me is that I lay down my life—only to take it up again. No one takes it from me, but I lay it down of my own accord.** *I have authority to lay it down and authority to take it up again. This command I received from my Father* (John 10:14-18 NIV).

Jesus willingly laid His life down for us, giving up His life so ours can be preserved through His precious blood being shed and the anointing that He gives us. This is why we must always forgive others, especially those who mistreat us because forgiveness is key to preserving the blessing of God on our lives. We are brought to the importance of this, when our Lord, who is full of compassion and mercy, instructs us to forgive those who wronged us in Luke 23:34 (NLT). It is the key for keeping the anointing of preservation upon us and imperative we walk in holiness before Him.

This is why Ecclesiastes 9:8 tells us to keep our garments always white and let not our heads lack any anointing. It is because our garments being white speaks of our lifestyle and the blessing that covers us in the anointing of preservation that is poured out upon us. This is why it is essential that believers live a life of holiness to keep the anointing and protection of God. Otherwise, as the story of Samson shows, there may be dire consequences if God's mantle is removed because of disobedience or sin.

We have discovered that it is the anointing that preserves you. So, how do you keep the anointing and even increase it? David provides us with answers in Psalm 15 (NLT):

Who may worship in your sanctuary, Lord? Who may enter your presence on your holy hill? Those who lead blameless lives and do what is right, speaking the truth from sincere hearts. Those who refuse to gossip or harm their neighbors or speak evil of their friends. Those who despise flagrant sinners, and honor the faithful followers of the Lord, and keep their promises even when it hurts. Those who lend money without charging interest, and who cannot be bribed to lie about the innocent. Such people will stand firm forever.

Staying connected to God and His anointing is one of the surest ways to protect and preserve your life. As with Jesus who spoke the Word, we must do the same, especially reading the Bible provides spiritual sustenance that increases your anointing. With this connection, you are truly empowered to live a victorious Christian life.

LIVE RIGHTEOUSLY

God's Word and Spirit keeps the anointing of preservation activated and empowered in our lives. However, it is preserved, kept by our lifestyle and choices we make. We must never forget that by connecting to unholy or sinful anointing or things, we open the door for the devil to attack.

Be sober, be vigilant; because your adversary the devil walks about like a roaring lion, seeking whom he may devour (1 Peter 5:8 NKJV).

The Amplified Bible makes that verse even more clear about how important it is to live a life that is self-disciplined, walking in what is right and holy before the Lord.

Be sober [well balanced and self-disciplined], be alert and cautious at all times. That enemy of yours, the devil, prowls around like a roaring lion [fiercely hungry], seeking someone to devour (1 Peter 5:8 AMP).

There are so many benefits, when we remain connected to godly and righteous living. It literally activates the anointing of preservation on us—just like Jesus did.

It is not just an obedient, holy lifestyle but also found in our decisions. I will tell you; I have found one decision in my life that has reaped decades of blessings and preservation. It might surprise you but is revealed to us in Scripture as a supernatural benefit. Are you ready? It is tithing, and it is a very important way to increase that anointing that preserves. It opens a supernatural connection in Heaven when we give into God's Kingdom, and it provides us active protection from whatever the enemy may try to do.

This is why Malachi chapter 3 says, that when we tithe and give to the Lord, it literally opens the windows of Heaven and God pours back blessings that we don't even have room to receive! Yet, that is not all! It is even connected to preservation. How is that you might ask? God promised to rebuke the devil who comes to devour when we tithe. Now that is preservation! We not only get profound abundant blessings but preservation as well. As we see in Scripture, lack of giving often leads only to poverty and hardship; but giving, especially tithing, activates a protective power that nullifies our adversary!

YOUR SUPERNATURAL COVERING NEUTRALIZES THE ENEMY.

Another powerful way to ensure the anointing of preservation is by connecting to the body of Christ, especially in regard to an anointed leader and church. When we do, we gain access to a special spiritual atmosphere, allowing us to encounter God powerfully in anointed worship, and gain insight from bold Holy Spirit sermons. In addition, it enables us to experience the supernatural power of God and form lasting relationships. With godly guidance from these beneficial facets of the church, you'll be able to avoid anything that might defile or dishonor your faith, thus increasing your own anointing for preservation.

> *Rightly did Isaiah prophesy about you hypo-crites (play-actors, pretenders), as it is written [in Scripture], "These people honor Me with their lips, but their heart is far from Me. They worship Me in vain [their worship is meaningless and worth-less, a pretense], teaching the precepts of men as doctrines [giving their traditions equal weight with the Scriptures]." You disregard and neglect the commandment of God, and cling [faithfully] to the tradition of men* (**Mark 7:6-8 AMP**).

Jesus continued, telling them what defiles and dishon-ors people—what brings them destruction:

> *For it is from within, out of a person's heart, that evil thoughts come—sexual immorality, theft, murder, adultery, greed, malice, deceit, lewd-ness, envy, slander, arrogance and folly. All these evils come from inside and defile a person* (**Mark 7:21-23 NIV**).

Paul confirms the necessity of having good associations with godly, anointed people who love the Lord and are connected to God and His Kingdom. Paul tells his protégé, Timothy:

> *As I urged you when I went into Macedonia, stay there in Ephesus so that you may* **command certain people not to teach false doctrines any longer or to devote themselves to myths and endless genealogies**. *Such things promote*

controversial speculations rather than advancing God's work—which is by faith. **The goal of this command is love, which comes from a pure heart and a good conscience and a sincere faith.** *Some have departed from these and have turned to meaningless talk. They want to be teachers of the law, but they do not know what they are talking about or what they so confidently affirm* (1 Timothy 1:3-7 NIV).

Increasing the anointing on you can be as simple as taking Paul's advice to the church in Philippi:

Finally, brothers and sisters, whatever is true, whatever is noble, whatever is right, whatever is pure, whatever is lovely, whatever is admirable— if anything is excellent or praiseworthy—think about such things (Philippians 4:8 NIV).

All these Scriptures are written for our admonishment, but also an example of how to protect the anointing of preservation upon our lives. It is as simple as staying connected to the right people, places, and things that preserve our lives and well-being. It gives no place to the enemy and causes a barrier to the enemies' attacks. There is power in connecting to the anointed body of Christ.

5

IDENTIFY
THE ENEMY

The thief [satan] *does not come except to steal,
and to kill, and to destroy. I* [Jesus] *have come
that they may have life, and that they may have
it more abundantly* (John 10:10 NKJV).

Jesus made it very clear in His statement recorded in John 10:10—satan is your enemy. Jesus is your Savior. The enemy, the devil wants nothing more than to steal preservation from you. He does it by stealing, killing, and destroying. The life that Jesus promised is an abundant life walking in the anointing of preservation. We must take authority over the enemy and not allow his tactics, we must resist him and he will flee—resulting in preservation.

To resist the devil and his attempts to steal, kill, and destroy, we identify his tactics and know who is out to get us. The Bible (NKJV) reveals the enemy throughout the Scriptures, labeling him:

accuser (Revelation 12:10)	**adversary** (Job 1)
antichrist (book of Revelation)	**baal** (Judges 2)
beast (book of Revelation)	**beelzebub** (Matthew 12:24)
belial (2 Corinthians 6:15)	**deceiver** (book of Revelation)
demon (Matthew 8:31-33)	**dragon** (Revelation 12)
enemy (Matthew 13:39)	**evildoer** (Isaiah 1:4)
wicked one (1 John 5:19)	**fallen angel/morning star** (Isaiah 14:12-15)
lawless one (2 Thessalonians 2:8-9)	**liar, father of lies** (John 8:44)
lucifer (Isaiah 14:12)	**murderer** (John 8:44)
prince of the power of the air (Ephesians 2:2)	**roaring lion** (1 Peter 5:8)
satan (book of Job)	**serpent** (Genesis 3)
thief, robber, destroyer (John 10:10)	**wicked one** (Matthew 13:19)

I believe that it saddens God when we blame Him for tragedies, calamities, sickness, or death that is actually caused by the devil. This is why in John 10:10, Jesus clearly distinguishes between the goodness of God and the evil of satan.

In clear terms, Jesus states that the devil is responsible for killing, stealing, and destroying while expressing that He is the Source of abundant life. As we have discovered in the biblical references in this book, by calling upon the name of the Lord, we can experience blessings, healing, protection, rescue, and preservation. Remember, this is our covenant rights package and the free gift given upon salvation, also known as *sozo*. Asserting your *sozo* rights, which come as part of your salvation, establishes you as a favored child of God, who must be aware of the enemy's attacks.

The enemy uses many things to lead people astray. The devil wants nothing more than for us to not know what Jesus paid for and what is legally ours in our covenant. If he can gain access in our lives and we open our hearts or lives to him, he gains access to steal the preservation of a blessed covenant life and all it entails. A good example would be with Judas, one of Jesus's disciples. He had every benefit as the others, but opened the door of his heart to the devil and his life was cut short. The anointing that preserved his life while serving under Jesus was sadly shortened as he took his own life.

> *Now the Festival of Unleavened Bread, called the Passover, was approaching, and the chief priests and the teachers of the law were looking for some way to get rid of Jesus, for they were afraid of the people. Then Satan entered Judas, called Iscariot, one of the Twelve. And Judas went*

to the chief priests and the officers of the temple guard and discussed with them how he might betray Jesus. They were delighted and agreed to give him money (Luke 22:1-5 NIV).

Judas's life was stolen from him by his own greed, affecting the anointing of preservation upon him. The enemy fears *who* we know, being Jesus, and *what* we know, being our covenant rights. He seeks to challenge both and look for an open door, seeking whom he may devour. Keep speaking the power of what Jesus provided, continue to boldly say, "The Spirit of the Lord is upon me. I am anointed," and you invite the power of God's Spirit into your life and activate the anointing of preservation. With this anointing present, you raise up a standard against the attacks of the devil, who will be restrained from laying his hands on you. Indeed, when you are anointed, you are shielded from the thief's schemes.

> *But in that coming day **no weapon turned against you will succeed**. You will silence every voice raised up to accuse you. These benefits are enjoyed by the servants of the Lord; their vindication will come from me. I, the Lord, have spoken!* (Isaiah 54:17 NLT)

By *"no weapon,"* it means absolutely none—not even the devil's most insidious tactics will succeed against you. We must not only believe this but claim it, declaring it in faith boldly! In addition, your detractors will be rendered speechless. I believe it can also mean that we should be wise and avoid getting into heated arguments, particularly on social media.

Jesus willingly endured ridicule, taunts, and misunderstandings but always stayed in the Spirit of love and truth, preserving His life until He laid it down. As representatives of God on earth, we can also deflect the devil's arrows and avoid getting into the flesh that opens us up for attacks from the enemy. Jesus specifically informed His disciples and us:

> *I tell you the truth, anyone who believes in me will do the same works I have done, and even greater works, because I am going to be with the Father. You can ask for anything in my name, and I will do it, so that the Son can bring glory to the Father. Yes, ask me for anything in my name, and I will do it!* **(John 14:12-14 NLT)**

If we want to see powerful results in our lives and concerning others, we must be like Jesus as Christians and believers in Him. Being a Christian means being Christlike and anointed. When we are saved, walking in the spirit, we become an anointed person, like Christ. We then are able to perform extraordinary works that bring honor to the Father, like Jesus did. We must be vigilant and able to recognize the enemy to avoid turning away from God's Word and living a life that affects the anointing of preservation upon us.

BY HIS SPIRIT

A vital way to protect us from the onslaughts of the enemy is for Christians to establish and maintain a connection to the anointing of God on our lives. One way we do this is through His Word, but also in regular fellowship with other believers under the guidance of anointed leadership. It helps to bring the anointing of preservation against the schemes and deceptions of the enemy. This is because whenever two or more gather in God's name, His presence is there with them (as demonstrated in Matthew 18:20, Ecclesiastes 4:9-12, Hebrews 10:25, Luke 8:4, among others). This presence comes because of our agreement, and God releases His spirit to go forth in power and demonstration. It is what the enemy fears as it exposes and destroys his assignments not in our ability, but by His Spirit.

> *So he answered and said to me: "This is the word of the Lord to Zerubbabel: 'Not by might nor by power, but by My Spirit,' says the Lord of hosts"* **(Zechariah 4:6 NKJV).**

When we try to do things in our own efforts or power, we will not succeed in overcoming the attacks of the enemy. Zechariah prophesies, essentially stating, "Take heed, you cannot succeed by mere human ability. Your victory comes not from your own power, nor strength, but through the Spirit." To be able to combat the devil, we must possess an anointing—it's that straightforward and miraculous. It is all about God and His Spirit. This was what caused Jesus to minister in such power and destroy the works of the devil, especially seeing many healed and touched by the anointing.

> And you know that **God anointed Jesus of Nazareth with the Holy Spirit and with power.** *Then Jesus went around doing good and healing all who were oppressed by the devil, for God was with him* (Acts 10:38 NLT).

The Holy Spirit is the ultimate Source of the anointing that preserves us. When His Spirit rests upon us, we become anointed for action demonstrated with His power. Jesus spent much of His time performing good deeds through the anointing of the Holy Spirit and healing those oppressed by the devil. It was the devil, not God, who was responsible for inflicting sickness and oppression upon people. Jesus was bold in His assignment to speak up and bold about His assignment to expose darkness and release an anointing to preserve the betterment of those He touched.

We as believers, especially leaders, need to do as Jesus did. He took a stand against evil by speaking up and distinguishing right from wrong. There is such a need for that today, especially in preserving the truth, maintaining a standard of righteousness and morals. Sadly, many people, even Christians, take a neutral approach or a cowardly approach to taking a stand against darkness and the things the enemy is trying to do, especially in our culture. Yet, we have an anointing to make a difference and to help preserve not only our lives but a generation.

This anointing is a power that does not come from our own selves but from the Holy Spirit, in His boldness. It is what is making a difference that we are seeing in this hour. Yet, there are always those who adopt the belief that "we should not confront darkness or the evils of our day" and especially they say, "avoid politics."

As I mentioned from the start of this book, we cannot remain silent or inactive or we will greatly hinder the anointing released to preserve our generation. We must refuse to be silent as I believe we are being summoned by God to stand boldly, courageously, and without fear in His anointing that destroys the works of darkness.

DO SOMETHING

I believe more than ever now is the time for Christians to act, or evil will prevail. In addition to prayer, we must stand up and declare our faith in Jesus as Lord. The more we expose the darkness and speak truth concerning the many lies of the devil, an anointing is released to bring preservation. The devil loses his strongholds and righteousness prevails.

It's critical that we understand and recognize the tactics of the devil. Lawlessness, lies, and deceptions are how he is trying to steal, kill, and destroy today.

> *The coming of the lawless one will be in accordance with how Satan works. He will use all sorts of displays of power through signs and wonders that serve the lie, and all the ways that*

wickedness deceives those who are perishing. They perish because they refused to love the truth and so be saved (2 Thessalonians 2:9-10 NIV).

In my conviction, had Jesus been present on earth today, He wouldn't be silent as some are, especially His preachers. I strongly believe if He was operating in His ministry during the years 2020-2022 as we saw many lies and attempts of the enemy to destroy the innocent and even our nation, He would have made the statement, "I came to do good and heal those oppressed by the devil, which is what I shall continue doing today. You will not close down My church, nor My ministry. You won't censor Me—and for the record, I will be performing good and healing tomorrow, the day after, and the next day as well." This would have been His message, and it should be ours as well—today and every day.

We are powerfully anointed by His Spirit to go about doing good and destroying the works of the devil. We are key to releasing the anointing of preservation that makes a difference in our lives. This is how our families, cities, regions, and nations will be gloriously changed and preserved. It is when we work with the Holy Spirit as His anointed vessels.

And they went forth, and preached every where, the Lord working with them, and confirming the word with signs following. Amen (Mark 16:20 KJV).

ANOINTED WORDS

As already explained, we usually associate the concept of the anointing solely with the laying on of hands or the transmission of physical mantles, as with Elijah and Elisha. However, in Matthew 8:5-13, we can see that Jesus was able to heal the centurion's servant by speaking the word only. This denotes that we, too, can unleash the power of the anointing through our words.

This is why I can't stress the importance of continuing to declare, "The Spirit of the Lord is upon me, I am anointed," to bring God's anointing into your life. We need to adopt the same faith standard and understanding of the centurion in the Bible that knew the power of words to make a difference. It not only healed his servant but preserved his life!

> *And Jesus saith unto him, I will come and heal him. The centurion answered and said, Lord, I am not worthy that thou shouldest come under my roof: but speak the word only, and my servant shall be healed* (Matthew 8:7-8 KJV).

I promise you, if you make a continued habit of saying and believing this truth, you will certainly see the benefits. Just think how much the enemy is fearing your words about the revelation concerning the anointing of preservation!

6

TRANSFIGURATION

Prayer: Father, may Your glory cover this earth as the waters cover the sea. Let there be greater measures of the glory that touches the United States, into Canada, down into Mexico, Central America, South America, Lord, over into the Caribbean and throughout the United Kingdom, into Europe, Russia, Africa, the Middle East, Asia, India, Australia, the islands of the sea, Lord. Let Your glory increase that a great awakening shall arise, Lord, people's eyes, their hearts, shall turn to You. Let the hour of transfiguration, Lord, of beautiful changes, sudden changes, come upon the earth to glorify You. Oh God, this I pray in Jesus's name. Thank You, Lord, for Your anointing.

Rather than beginning with a Bible verse, this chapter opens with a prayer. It is a plea for God's anointing to come and cover the earth, so that His glory may be seen by all.

What if we were able to understand the future? Not in some vague, psychic way—but truly comprehend it through our spirit and the Spirit of God? Jesus often asked those around Him why they did not "understand" His words. In Matthew 16 He posed this question, *"Don't you understand even yet? Don't you remember the 5,000 I fed with five loaves, and the baskets of leftovers you picked up?"* Here Jesus is referencing a miracle He performed earlier in which He used only five loaves of bread to feed 5,000 people. By understanding this divine power, we can gain insight into the potential possibilities that the Spirit of God holds.

> *Don't you understand even yet? Don't you remember the 5,000 I fed with five loaves, and the baskets of leftovers you picked up? Or the 4,000 I fed with seven loaves, and the large baskets of leftovers you picked up? Why can't you understand that I'm not talking about bread? So again I say, "Beware of the yeast of the Pharisees and Sadducees"* (Matthew 16:9-11 NLT).

Finally, the disciples came to the realization that Jesus was speaking of more than just bread—He was talking about the false teachings of the Pharisees and Sadducees.

We should take note of all the questions Jesus posed in Scripture, as they are still relevant today. When He asked His followers if they believed He could miraculously feed thousands with almost no food, they simply couldn't grasp that God's supernatural power was right in front of them.

Our natural understanding will only get us so far—too often we limit ourselves and neglect to consider how much further we can go. Reflecting on Jesus's words reminds us that sometimes our faith needs to supersede our logical minds. To this day He continues to ask people, "Do you believe?"

> *And when He had come into the house, the blind men came to Him. And Jesus said to them, "**Do you believe** that I am able to do this?" They said to Him, "Yes, Lord"* (Matthew 9:28 NKJV).

> *Jesus answered and said to him, "Because I said to you, 'I saw you under the fig tree,' **do you believe?** You will see greater things than these"* (John 1:50 NKJV).

> *And whoever lives and believes in Me shall never die. **Do you believe** this?* (John 11:26 NKJV).

> ***Do you not believe** that I am in the Father, and the Father in Me? The words that I speak to you I do not speak on My own authority; but the Father who dwells in Me does the works* (John 14:10 NKJV).

> *Jesus answered them, "**Do you now believe**?"* (John 16:31)

An invalid man had been at the pool of Bethesda for 38 years, desperately hoping that he would finally be able to enter and be healed. Yet due to his condition, he was always pushed out of the way by others. But then Jesus asked him a question, *"Do you want to get well?"* (John 5:6 NIV).

This same question can still be heard echoing throughout the world today—do we truly believe that Jesus can heal us and that available through Him is an anointing that preserves? Despite our situations, many of us keep trying to find our answers on our own. But Jesus is continuously asking us if we have faith in His ability to make us better.

What do you believe? Do you comprehend the meaning of why Christ went to the cross—for our healing and full benefits package of blessings. In addition, He has granted us the anointing of His Holy Spirit's power, including preservation? Are you aware that there is a divine stirring in your spirit leading you to believe in Jesus, God's one and only Son, for more of what has been provided through your covenant and His anointing? (See John 3:16.)

If so, then I'm here to assure you that things will get better. The tumultuous darkness we have faced will turn into light. A global revival is nearing. This generation, our lives, and our nation is being gloriously preserved through His anointing that has been released. When Jesus asks if we have faith in Him and understand the future He holds, let us respond with confidence, "Yes! I believe! God, I understand You are at work among us!"

For those who have felt trapped in a cycle of despair and hardship for years, constantly hearing that this is the "new norm," I'm here to tell you that God has something else for you. If you believe in Him, all the years of suffering and lack of understanding can be wiped away. Jesus is calling out to you right now—open your heart and accept His love, and His goodness will transform your life in an instant. Believe.

TIMES OF TRANSFIGURATION

I heard the Lord say to me, "Times of transfiguration are coming now."

"Lord, what is transfiguration?"

He said, "You're actually in the process of it."

I always thought I understood the meaning of "transfiguration," but looking it up revealed a much richer definition. "Transfiguration means a change in form or appearance; an exalting, glorifying, or spiritual change." In the same way, God is leading us toward a better, more beautiful existence than we are experiencing now—in ourselves, our nation, and our world. This is happening through His anointing that preserves!

> *After six days Jesus took Peter, James and John with him and led them up a high mountain, where they were all alone. There he was transfigured before them. His clothes became dazzling white, whiter than anyone in the world could bleach them* (Mark 9:2-3 NIV).

Jesus's transfiguration was the result of the glory and visible presence of God. When we call on God's glory and anointing, we can expect to experience changes in our lives and a powerful sense of His presence around us.

TAKE A DEEP BREATH, JUST SIGH.

I believe the Lord saying, "Tell everyone to take a deep breath and sigh. Take a moment to do that now—inhale deeply and release it slowly. Let out a sigh of relief, for with this transfiguration comes the sound of justice and the voice of truth, growing ever louder." That sigh is a sigh of relief.

After taking a few deep breaths and sighs, say to the Lord, "Lord God, Your Spirit is upon me. I am anointed. The Spirit of the Lord is upon me. I'm anointed with the anointing of preservation. I will live long. I live strong. I live healthily. I live with hope that things are changing in my life, for those I love, and for this nation and the nations of the earth. Lord, it is because of the covenants I have with You through Your blood, Jesus, and with the Holy Spirit of promise. I'm sealed with the Holy Spirit of promise. And part of that seal is the anointing that is upon me of preservation."

> *...in whom also after that ye believed, ye were sealed with that holy Spirit of promise* (Ephesians 1:13 KJV).

PRESERVATION AND HEALING

This seal of the Holy Spirit is the anointing that preserves our lives, our health, our family, and so much more. The anointing of preservation is not just about protecting our lives only from the wiles of the devil but also to preserve our lives, so we can live healthy and strong. If we want true transfiguration or change, we can't live outside of what Jesus provided in the shedding of His blood. We must not come into agreement with a sinful life, or a life that is contrary to our covenant benefits. When we do, it greatly affects the anointing of preservation that is upon us.

Too many accept life as it comes and struggle to live the abundant life Jesus promised. It really comes down to what we come into agreement with and who we come into agreement with. We either come into agreement with God and His Word—or the enemy and his evil attacks. This is why we must not come into agreement with sickness or things trying to attack our body or our loved ones. We must never tolerate the enemy trying to invade our lives! We must never tolerate the devil and his attacks against what Jesus paid for through His blood, including our health, our soundness of mind, our well-being and prosperity. Never let him violate your covenant rights.

Instead, let's continue to watch the anointing of preservation at work as we come into agreement with God, His Word, and the covenant He has provided. We will then gloriously see the results of a healthy, long, and strong life being preserved upon this earth.

Jesus says in Matthew 18:19 (NKJV):

Again I say to you that if two of you agree on earth concerning anything that they ask, it will be done for them by My Father in heaven.

I urge you to lift your hand and wave it and say, "I come into agreement with Jesus, His Word and the powerful covenant He provided through His blood. I command that the hordes of hell, every demon spirit, and the devil himself can go to the dry places and to the pit of hell concerning me, my life, my loved ones, and all that concerns me. I don't receive sickness. I don't receive disease. I don't receive even allergies. I don't receive any pain, tragedy, or calamity. I don't receive any of that. I put it under my feet. I reject it. I resist it. It's not my covenant right. Jesus paid for my healing, my protection, and all the benefits of my covenant. The Holy Spirit is upon me, and I am preserved by my covenant with Him and His anointing!"

In fact, right now, I speak over you and release that anointing now that preserves, declaring it breaks every generational curse of heredity, infirmity, sickness, and disease. I declare, you are *not* subject to the sicknesses, diseases, infirmities, or tragedies, calamity of prior generations. It is cut off by the covenant of His blood. I decree that you receive your covenant right as the family of God—all generational iniquity and all generational infirmity is broken because Jesus's sacrifice became that curse, and now you are the blessing and live in the blessing to the fullest. Therefore, all illness must come out of your body and not touch you again and every assignment is destroyed, and every heavy burden is undone through His anointing. In the name of Yeshua!

Always remember the power of agreement with God and what He has provided. It is the key of preservation in all areas. Continue to say no to the devil—and say yes to receiving healing and all good and great things the Lord has for you.

Keep releasing the anointing that is upon you when you declare it! Speak the Word of God and faith-filled words! Remember, the Word is anointed because Jesus is the Word and the Word was with God, and the Word was God and the Word became flesh and dwelt among us. God has given us His Spirit-inspired Word. It came as men were moved upon by the Holy Spirit, they began to write and declare the Holy Scriptures. The Word is anointed. This is why we see results and the anointing of preservation released! This is why we can continue to see a life preserved from sickness and disease.

I encourage you to continue to stand strong for what is rightfully yours or what you are standing and believing for others. If it is to see your life or the life of someone else touched and healed by God, lift up your voice and use the very power and authority the Lord has given you. Begin declaring right now, "Lord, You were wounded, Jesus, for our transgressions. You were bruised for our iniquities. You took the chastisement. You took our punishment, so that by Your stripes, those whips upon Your bleeding back as the powers plowed Your back, making deep, long their furrows, we are healed. Thank You, Lord. Amen, it is done!"

7

GOD'S SECRETS

Surely the Lord God does nothing, unless He reveals His
secret to His servants the prophets (Amos 3:7 NKJV).

Prophets are vessels of God's prophetic secrets, and only He determines when they are to be shared. Prophets simply share the Lord's heart and must wait on Him to know when those secrets are to be shared. This is what makes true prophecy from the office of the prophet so powerful as it comes from God's heart revealed to them. This means the Lord shares His heart, mind, will, feelings, and agenda to His servants the prophets, according to the Scripture.

> *Surely the Lord God will do nothing, but he revealeth his secret unto his servants the prophets* (Amos 3:7 KJV).

True prophets of the Lord are the friends and servants of the Lord. He uses them when He desires to do something on earth; and as the Scripture mentions, will do nothing until it is revealed to them and through them. The prophets of the Lord throughout the Bible held a sacred place in the heart of God and as seen in Scripture. They would often prophesy what seemed to contradict current conditions and inevitably met with criticism and even death. Despite this, their words came to pass, displaying the power of God's word spoken through them.

God will frequently speak of events before they transpire. This is how He reveals His heart and will to those on earth. Through prophecy, He releases a prophetic sound that must precede what He says. In other words, He announces it first before it manifests. For instance, when God speaks of coming changes in certain areas, He gives notice beforehand.

Sound always precedes the manifestation of events. We see this in the beginning of creation in the book of Genesis; when God said let there be light, it released a sound from His words and then brought the manifestation into being. *"Let there be light,"* and then the light appeared (Genesis 1:3 NIV). The same is true in all areas; before something manifests, it must first be spoken into existence.

This is why we have learned the importance of declaring, "The Spirit of the Lord is upon me and I am anointed with His anointing of preservation." When we declare it, the result is, it happens! This same principle is true regarding the prophetic anointing, the prophetic office and how God uses it to preserve a people and a nation. When prophecy goes forth, and a true prophet declares God's word, it happens! This is how God brings His will, His plan to earth and releases preservation through His anointing. It is why God is still using the prophetic office and anointing on earth today.

Whenever you hear prophecies, it is a sign that something from God is about to manifest. This is seen in Luke 1 when the angel told Mary she would give birth to the Son of the Lord. Although it had not yet come to pass, God had shared His secret with His angel, and so Mary was prophesying what would happen in the future. Ultimately, Jesus was born on earth as God had said, following His sound coming before manifestation.

The prophet Isaiah spoke of, prophesied the coming Messiah hundreds of years before Jesus walked on the earth. Isaiah 53 in part says:

> *Surely He has borne our griefs and carried our sorrows; yet we esteemed Him stricken, smitten by God, and afflicted. But He was wounded for our transgressions, He was bruised for our iniquities; the chastisement for our peace was upon Him, and by His stripes we are healed. All we like sheep have gone astray; we have turned, every one, to his own way; and the Lord has laid on Him the iniquity of us all* (Isaiah 53:4-6 NKJV).

Isaiah provided a glimpse into the future, predicting not only the coming of Jesus but also His purpose. He spoke of how Jesus would bring us comfort, bear our sorrows, heal us, and take away all our sins. The Lord continues in this day to share His heart, His secrets of what is to come through His prophets, and His word does indeed come to pass.

The role of the prophet throughout Scripture is evident. They carried God's secrets and the Lord would do nothing without revealing His heart, His secrets to them first before manifesting those prophetic words on earth. The prophets stood with kings, helped govern nations, guided the Lord's people through challenges and dark times, even giving warnings to preserve them. This has not changed today. The Lord has given prophets that Jesus chose as it pleased Him and set them in the church (Ephesians 4:11 and 1 Corinthians 12:28).

If you are desiring to know more about true prophecy or true prophets and how they function today, let me encourage you to get my book I wrote on this subject titled, *Throne Room Prophecy: Your Guide to Accurately Discerning the Word of the Lord.* It will help you immensely and show you just how sacred God's heart is and how we must steward over it with honor and reverence in regard to prophecy and true prophets.

CLOSE TO HOME

Let's go on a journey back to August 2020. I'll never forget that moment. I was working on my HO train layout in my basement when I felt the presence of God enter the room. I immediately stopped what I was doing and said, "Lord, You're here." It was one of the most precious moments that ever happened to me. I realized what a beautiful Person our Lord is and the demonstration of love He has for us.

Then I heard the voice of God say, "May I speak to you?" As I stood there feeling His presence, I fell to my knees onto the floor, my face bowed forward. I was shaking. I felt a holy reverence in His presence. I said, "God, Your servant hears, and whatever You say to me, if You desire, I shall repeat Your words, otherwise I will hold Your secret within my heart."

The Lord told me that things will be done to alter the outcome of the US presidential election. He then revealed to me that He would use the election to get His harvest, and we would see His hand over our nation that would bring honor to His Son, Jesus. He was very determined about the children of this generation and dealing with the enemy, who is trying to steal their future. He told me the enemy would *not* succeed in taking this nation from Him. I asked the Lord why, and how this was possible. I will never forget what He replied. He said, "Because of the anointing of preservation that is upon this land."

Those prophetic words shook me, and I believe with all my heart that we are and will continue to see those words come to pass. I felt so humbled the Lord would share His secrets of what He is doing in this nation, especially to preserve it through His anointing! We need to be encouraged by those words as we must always remember that it was through a prophetic anointing and a prophet that the nation Israel was preserved. Praise God it is the same way He is preserving this nation today!

> *And by a prophet the Lord brought Israel out of Egypt, and by a prophet was he preserved* (Hosea 12:13 KJV).

So many have been through great battles, even this nation and the nations of the earth. Yet I have come to understand that conflict can be a source of strength, which is why the devil was so foolish when he tempted Jesus in the wilderness. For forty days and nights, satan did not realize that this confrontation would bring forth the power of the Holy Spirit onto Jesus and cause Him to triumph.

The scene between the devil and Jesus is told in Luke 4:1-14: *"**Jesus, being filled with the Holy Spirit**, returned from the Jordan [where He had been baptized] and was led by the Spirit into the wilderness.... Then Jesus returned in the **power of the Spirit** to Galilee...."* Jesus came out of those 40 days of temptation with the power of the Spirit of God upon Him.

So, what does this mean for us? We've experienced some recent years of difficult circumstances and upheaval. The enemy thought he could crush God's people and His church, but our all-knowing Lord was saying all along that when we are walking in His will, the devil cannot succeed. He tempted Jesus and instead of succumbing, Jesus gained even more power and strength. I believe the same is true for this nation. God is not done—we are being preserved for His final harvest and for the children of this generation. Don't lose hope, don't give up, and certainly don't believe the lies that are being told throughout the earth today.

We are going to see transfiguration in this nation and the nations of this world. We are going to see change. We are going to see God's glory—and we are going to see His power. That's what all the turmoil and trouble will produce. And part of the change that will take place is because of the anointing of preservation—God has preserved the blessing, anointing, and freedom that is the foundation of the United States.

> *For the Lord is the Spirit, and wherever the Spirit of the Lord is, there is freedom* (**2 Corinthians 3:17 NLT**).

The anointing of preservation will end the suffering that has gripped our nation. The enemy thought he could create a "new normal" for us, but only God can truly create—and He crafted His perfect redemptive plan from the start. Through this conflict, God is about to bring an anointing that will cause the world to marvel in awe.

JESUS FULFILLS SCRIPTURE

After Jesus left the wilderness, He moved from place to place sharing His knowledge and demonstrating the anointing of the Holy Spirit in synagogues across the region. People were amazed at His knowledge and the power with which He taught. On one Sabbath day, He was in His hometown of Nazareth and read from the book of Isaiah—a passage that stunned everyone with its power. Let's take a moment to read it again together; it is truly remarkable!

> *So He* [Jesus] *came to Nazareth, where He had been brought up. And as His custom was, He went into the synagogue on the Sabbath day, and stood up to read. And He was handed the book of the prophet Isaiah. And when He had*

opened the book, He found the place where it was written:

"The Spirit of the Lord is upon Me, because He has anointed Me to preach the gospel to the poor; He has sent Me to heal the brokenhearted, to proclaim liberty to the captives and recovery of sight to the blind, to set at liberty those who are oppressed; to proclaim the acceptable year of the Lord."

Then He closed the book, and gave it back to the attendant and sat down. And the eyes of all who were in the synagogue were fixed on Him. And He began to say to them, "Today this Scripture is fulfilled in your hearing" **(Luke 4:16-21 NKJV).**

Jesus proclaims that God has anointed Him to spread the Good News to the needy, heal the brokenhearted, bring freedom to those enslaved by darkness, give sight to the blind, and liberate the oppressed. The Spirit of the Lord rests on Him, releasing the presence and anointing of God which enables Jesus to fulfill His mission here, just as it is done in Heaven.

Then something incredible happened. Jesus rolled up the scroll, handed it to the attendant, and took His seat. Everyone in the synagogue was watching Him intently when He declared, *"Today this Scripture has been fulfilled right before your eyes."* These words that were spoken by Isaiah centuries ago were describing Him—Jesus the Messiah, God's Son! It must have been an electric moment for everyone in attendance.

Jesus may have been thinking, *Perfect, I have their focus. Now I can proceed to preach about the Kingdom of God.* He enjoyed being able to command attention and then use it to bring people the Good News. During His time on earth, Jesus encountered a lot of opposition for speaking the truth of the gospel.

> *Then he [Jesus] said, "You will undoubtedly quote me this proverb: 'Physician, heal yourself'— meaning, 'Do miracles here in your hometown like those you did in Capernaum.' But I tell you the truth, no prophet is accepted in his own hometown. Certainly there were many needy widows in Israel in Elijah's time, when the heavens were closed for three and a half years, and a severe famine devastated the land. Yet Elijah was not sent to any of them. He was sent instead to a foreigner—a widow of Zarephath in the land of Sidon. And many in Israel had leprosy in the time of the prophet Elisha, but the only one healed was Naaman, a Syrian"* (Luke 4:23-27 NLT).

Mark 6:1-6 (NKJV) reveals the scene in the synagogue after Jesus's declaration:

> *Then He [Jesus] went out from there and came to His own country, and His disciples followed Him. And when the Sabbath had come, He began to teach in the synagogue. And many hearing Him were astonished, saying, "Where did this Man get these things? And what*

*wisdom is this which is given to Him, that such mighty works are performed by His hands! Is this not the carpenter, the Son of Mary, and brother of James, Joses, Judas, and Simon? And are not His sisters here with us?" So **they were offended at Him.***

*But Jesus said to them, "A prophet is not without honor except in his own country, among his own relatives, and in his own house." Now **He could do no mighty work there, except that He laid His hands on a few sick people and healed them**. And He marveled because of their unbelief. Then He went about the villages in a circuit, teaching.*

There is something that can hinder the anointing and the anointing of preservation—familiarity, and it is the enemy of the anointing. Familiarity is why Jesus as a Prophet was not received in His hometown and the reason some today are unable to understand prophetic words or the vessels that speak them. Familiarity causes people to reject the message, the messenger, thus affecting the desire of God to bless and preserve a nation and a people.

We see this familiarity when the people murmured and questioned Jesus's declaration. After all, wasn't He just a carpenter, the son of Mary? How could He know such things? Likewise, I believe congregations can get too familiar with their pastors. I caution pastors: Don't get too familiar with your church or the anointing power can be quenched. Even Jesus *"could do no mighty work there."*

That's the power of familiarity. They took a Man with unfathomable anointing and restricted it because of their lack of faith and comfort around Him. They scoffingly said, essentially, "He's just Joseph's son, the son of Mary; His siblings are just like us." Through their disbelief, they carelessly disregarded Jesus's boundless anointing to meet their needs.

Ponder this thought. Jesus was so anointed with preservation that He told God in the garden, *"During my time here, I protected them by the power of the name you gave me. I guarded them so that not one was lost, except the one headed for destruction, as the Scriptures foretold"* (John 17:12 NLT). The *"one headed for destruction"* was Judas, of course. But Jesus's anointing was safeguarding Judas until Judas got caught up in familiarity and a thirst for money.

> *Immediately Judas went to Jesus and said, "Greetings (rejoice), Rabbi!" And he kissed Him [in a deliberate act of betrayal]. Jesus said to Judas, "Friend, do what you came for." Then they came and seized Jesus and arrested Him* (Matthew 26:49-50 AMP).

The kiss of Jesus's close friend betrayed Him. When Judas kissed Jesus on the cheek, Judas's anointing faded away and the devil of suicide overtook him and killed him.

This is how powerful the anointing is in your life. That's why, if you are a minister, do not act carelessly. The anointing is sacred and priceless. The same applies to all—cherish

God's anointing on your life as something of great worth and sustaining power.

> *Through the power of the Holy Spirit who lives within us, carefully guard the precious truth that has been entrusted to you* (**2 Timothy 1:14 NLT**).

Going back to Luke 4, Jesus essentially said this, "Pay attention. Here I am in front of you. I am the Messiah and Anointed Prophet, and yet you reject Me. So now I'll go to the Gentiles." He made a key point here. He underlined that while lepers, widows, and a famine existed, God sent prophets to Zarephath the widow and Naaman the Syrian, both being Gentiles so their lives could be blessed and preserved. What happened then?

> *When they heard this,* **the people in the synagogue were furious**. *Jumping up, they mobbed him and forced him to the edge of the hill on which the town was built. They* **intended to push him over the cliff***, but* **he passed right through** *the crowd and went on his way* (Luke 4:28-30 NLT).

I'm telling you, Jesus made people angry with the truth. A great preacher will do the same thing. That's because when the truth is revealed, it does not just set you free, it confronts your heart and changes you. This might be uncomfortable at first, but it'll work out for the best in the end.

The people wanted to kill Jesus, and they were intent on throwing Him off a cliff. However, He managed to pass through the midst of them and kept going! How was this possible? It was due to the anointing of preservation. Jesus passed through the raging mob unscathed because He had been anointed to be protected in order to accomplish greater acts of God.

> *Therefore when Jesus perceived that they were about to come and take Him by force to make Him king, He departed again to the mountain by Himself alone. Now when evening came, His disciples went down to the sea, got into the boat, and went over the sea toward Capernaum. And* ***it was already dark, and Jesus had not come to them***. *Then the sea arose because a great wind was blowing. So when they had rowed about three or four miles, they saw Jesus walking on the sea and drawing near the boat; and* ***they were afraid***. *But He said to them, "It is I; do not be afraid." Then they willingly received Him into the boat, and immediately the boat was at the land where they were going* (**John 6:15-21 NKJV**).

I love this story because this is where I believe the United States of America is right now.

Jesus is praying and His disciples are out in a boat on the sea, headed toward Capernaum. It's dark outside, just like it is for some today who feel scared and think, *Oh no, it's dark. We can't do anything good now. All we can do is hope and pray that the Lord will take us up to Heaven.*

The New Living Translation puts the scene this way:

> *Soon a gale swept down upon them, and the sea grew very rough. They had rowed three or four miles when suddenly they saw Jesus walking on the water toward the boat. They were terrified, but he called out to them, "Don't be afraid. I am here!" Then they were eager to let him in the boat, and immediately they arrived at their destination!* (John 6:18-21 NLT)

This is where people are today—in fear and terror. "Oh, it's so dark and there's all kinds of shortages and inflation, high gas and food prices, a war going on and chaos in the streets." The darkness keeps spreading more dread. Jesus saw the disciples from the place of prayer at a time of darkness. He also sees the United States now.

In times of trouble and darkness, God shows up:

- **Deuteronomy 4:11 (NIV)** tells us that God was in the *"black clouds and deep darkness"* when He called Moses.

- **Genesis 1:1-3 (NIV)** says that the earth formless and empty and dark. Yet, *"God said, 'Let there be light,' and there was light."*

- **John 1:4-5 (NIV)** reveals that in Jesus is *"life and that life was the light of all mankind. The light shines in the darkness, and the darkness has not overcome it."*

- **2 Samuel 22:29 (NIV)** says, *"You, Lord, are my lamp; the Lord turns my darkness into light."*

- **Job 12:22 (NIV)** tells us that God *"reveals the deep things of darkness and brings utter darkness into the light."*

- **Psalm 112:4** comforts us with knowing that *"Even in darkness light dawns for the upright, for those who are gracious and compassionate and righteous."*

Isaiah especially provokes thoughts of America today and how some are clinging to lies:

> *Woe to those who call evil good and good evil, who put darkness for light and light for darkness, who put bitter for sweet and sweet for bitter* **(Isaiah 5:20 NIV).**

> *Then they will look toward the earth and see only distress and darkness and fearful gloom, and they will be thrust into utter darkness* **(Isaiah 8:22 NIV).**

Yet there is hope!

- God says, *"I will lead the blind by ways they have not known, along unfamiliar paths I will guide them; I will turn the darkness into light before them and make the rough places smooth. These are the things I will do; I will not forsake them"* (Isaiah 42:16 NIV). *"I form the light and create darkness, I bring prosperity and create disaster; I, the Lord, do all these things"* (Isaiah 45:7 NIV).

- Jesus tells us, *"I am the light of the world. Whoever follows me will never walk in darkness, but will have the light of life"* (John 8:12 NIV).

- And the apostle Paul writes, *"For God, who said, 'Let light shine out of darkness,' made his light shine in our hearts to give us the light of the knowledge of God's glory displayed in the face of Christ"* (2 Corinthians 4:6 NIV).

We need to be encouraged as God is intervening in these times of darkness. Light is overcoming the darkness, good is overcoming evil and our lives, our nation is being set up for God's finest hour! How is the Lord going to continue to intervene, to turn things around and preserve us and this nation? It is going to be through us and in addition by His servants the prophets who are not speaking words of doom, gloom, darkness, or negativity—but rather they are declaring the Spirit of the Lord is upon them, this nation, and the nations of the earth. We are being used by God to release His anointing of preservation.

The present and future could not look brighter!

8

A TEST?

Jesus soon saw a huge crowd of people coming to look for him. Turning to Philip, he asked, "Where can we buy bread to feed all these people?" He was testing Philip, for he already knew what he was going to do (John 6:5-6 NLT).

The New International Version of the Bible says of the scene in the middle of the lake:

Later that night, the boat was in the middle of the lake, and he **[Jesus]** *was alone on land. He saw the disciples straining at the oars, because the wind was against them. Shortly before dawn he went out to them, walking on the lake.* **He was about to pass by them**, *but when they saw him walking on the lake, they thought he was a ghost. They cried out, because they all saw him and were terrified* (Mark 6:47-50).

Did Jesus mean to pass by the boat? Was He intending to leave His disciples stranded in the middle of a raging storm? The New Living Translation says, *"He had intended to pass them by."* This was intentional on Jesus's part to see how His disciples would react and what their perspective would be by His visitation in the time of darkness. Yet, all the disciples could see were their desperate circumstances, instead of seeing that their Savior was coming right toward them in a powerful, supernatural visitation!

Sound familiar today as to how some are discerning the times and how their perspectives have been affected by lies and darkness? This is what people have been doing for the past two or more years and are still doing across the country. They watch news programs showing disturbing images and sensationalizing anything to stir up negative feelings—and taking it all as truth.

Yet, they can't discern we are in a time of visitation when the Lord is pouring out His Spirit and we are being preserved for something greater. Are we going to let this visitation pass us by like the disciples almost did, or are we going to continue to cry out to the Lord in the days that may seem evil?

The disciples called Jesus a "ghost." Although He was walking out on the water to save them in a visitation, all they could see was something evil coming to get them.

I think we're being tested right now. How much do we crave Jesus? How much do we long for God? When the disciples glimpsed Jesus walking on the sea, they assumed He was a ghost. Just stop there. He was in the process of visiting them, however they couldn't see it!

Nowadays when people focus on all the negative stuff—gas and food prices, inflation, the virus, etc.—they take note of the dark and ghostly aspect, the evil side of things. They don't realize that Jesus is right there alongside us; that it is a visitation from God Himself. Even Christians tend to attribute everything to evil, thus averting their attention away from God, Jesus, and the Holy Spirit who lives within them.

FOCUS ON GOD'S GOODNESS, NOT EVIL.

Don't be like the disciples. They can't see their redemption arriving. They can't see deliverance for their nation. They can't anticipate a spiritual reset for our planet. They can't perceive the glory right before them. All of this is replaced by an ominous presence—a frightful specter to them. All they foresee is doom and destruction.

This is the reality for many within this country today. They have accepted, and even embraced, the premise of a so-called new norm. Prices don't appear to be going down anytime soon. There doesn't seem to be any end in sight for restoring law and order on our streets and in our government. Mandates remain in place with no timeframe for their conclusion. Wars seem to go on indefinitely, and the list seems to go on and on.

Yet God is saying, "The great I AM visited a boat in the time of darkness and accelerated it to its destination. I can accelerate this nation as well, and I will."

I believe we are in the middle of the Lord's visitation in a time of darkness. Prophecies are being fulfilled.

All of what is happening today is because Jesus is coming with righteousness and justice. Where is our attention? On the chaos or the One who calms the seas?

> They had rowed three or four miles when suddenly they saw Jesus walking on the water toward the boat. They were terrified, but he called out to them, "Don't be afraid. I am here!" Then they were eager to let him in the boat, and immediately they arrived at their destination! (John 6:19-21 NLT)

Notice that "*the disciples were terrified, but **Jesus called out to them**.*" When we are terrified, afraid, worried, and confused, Jesus will call out to us. We must be focused on Him, not the circumstances.

When Jesus got into the boat, "*immediately they arrived at their destination!*" That's the supernatural anointing of preservation! From the middle of the lake, which took them three to four hours of rowing time, to immediately, miraculously, supernaturally arriving at the shore. I believe this is preserved outcome for you and I and this nation and the nations of the earth! We are in a time of visitation, and an anointing is released for that very purpose. Oh how we must not miss this day of visitation and realize we are being visited by God's Spirit.

What has been a harsh season of darkness and evil that has affected many, will in an instant suddenly change, as happened with the disciples on the lake. We will arrive as a people and a nation to what God intended, but we cannot get caught up in the darkness, deceived by or confused by what is really happening. Instead, we must summon the Lord into our lives and nation and watch how things suddenly, miraculously change, discovering just how much we are being blessed and preserved for His glory.

IMMEDIATELY THEY ARRIVED!

This is America's challenge—will we let Jesus pass us by or cry out to Him?

> *Then they willingly received Him into the boat, and immediately the boat was at the land where they were going* (John 6:21 NKJV).

The disciples welcomed Jesus into the boat. They knew He was their Savior and wanted Him with them.

Are we as a nation ready to accept Jesus into our churches, society, schools, places of work—and into our own lives? If not, it could be the reason behind the current turmoil. But when we willingly receive Him in these places and in our individual lives, He will take us away from any difficulties we are facing.

This is why we must rightfully discern what the Lord is doing, this brings protection and preservation and the anointing the Lord is releasing. He tells us not to be afraid, and yet we are still scared. But we should not be—Jesus rebukes storms and mobs alike. Let us remember how His anointing of preservation saved Him from the crowd that wanted to throw Him off a cliff. In the same way, the efforts of evildoers and those who cooperate with darkness will not succeed against us who are anointed with the anointing of preservation in this hour!

GOD'S HAND OF PROTECTION

Let's look at Psalm 89 to see again in a different context how the anointing and protection-preservation go together: *"I have found My servant David; with **My holy oil I have anointed him**, with whom My hand shall be established; also My arm shall strengthen him"* (Psalm 89:20-21 NKJV).

The Lord told Samuel to anoint David with oil, and from that day on the Spirit of the Lord was upon David.

> *Now the Lord said to Samuel, "How long will you mourn for Saul, seeing I have rejected him from*

reigning over Israel? **Fill your horn with oil, and go**; *I am sending you to Jesse the Bethlehemite. For I have provided Myself a king among his sons." ...Then* **Samuel took the horn of oil and anointed him** *in the midst of his brothers; and* **the Spirit of the Lord came upon David from that day forward**. *So Samuel arose and went to Ramah. ...Then one of the servants answered and said, "Look, I have seen a son of Jesse the Bethlehemite, who is skillful in playing, a mighty man of valor, a man of war, prudent in speech, and a handsome person; and* **the Lord is with him**" (1 Samuel 16:1,13,18 NKJV).

The anointing blessed David, turning him into a valiant and powerful young man—the one who defeated Goliath not just by a rock but by the anointing. So much that the same anointing that took Goliath out brought victory and preservation to a nation, Israel. It was through that anointing that David accomplished many other supernatural feats in God's service. Thanks to the anointing, he was strengthened, protected, and kept safe for what God had called him to do.

When you say the Spirit of the Lord is upon you, recognize that it is an honor and privilege. Do not take it lightly—it could mean the difference between life and death one day.

REST ASSURED YOU ARE PROTECTED AND WILL PREVAIL.

Let's continue to further discuss how the anointing kept Jesus from being harmed—no one laid a hand on Him (John 7:19-31). It protected Him until the time of His crucifixion. I want to dive deeper into this because our lives and well-being depends upon our understanding of it. We should strive to be like Jesus in this regard—when we know we have God's anointing of preservation upon us, we can rest easy knowing that we are shielded and given strength to persevere.

Allow me to show you how the anointing of preservation was removed in order for Jesus to be crucified, as this will give you faith in its power in your own life.

I love the discourse in John 8:56-58 (AMP) between Jesus and the Jewish leaders:

> "Your father Abraham [greatly] rejoiced to see My day (My incarnation). He saw it and was delighted." Then the Jews said to Him, "You are not even fifty years old, and You [claim to] have seen Abraham?" Jesus replied, "I assure you and most solemnly say to you, before Abraham was born, I Am."

Jesus, I just have to say, You are so amazing. I love Your sense of humor, and I love the way You mess with Your accusers. Jesus always gets the last laugh. The next verse tells us that the Jewish leaders *"Took up stones to throw at Him; but Jesus hid Himself and went out of the temple, going through the midst of them, and so passed by"* (John 8:59 NKJV). They thought Jesus was a false prophet and were ready to kill Him. But they couldn't figure out where He went. Because of the anointing, I can almost hear the leaders looking at each other and saying, "Dude, where'd He go? I was aiming right at Him with these stones, and then He was gone. Let's get back to the temple and find Him. Hurry!"

Jesus had hidden Himself and then passed right by them—supernaturally.

> **Then the Jews took up stones again to stone Him**. *Jesus answered them, "Many good works I have shown you from My Father. For which of those works do you stone Me?" The Jews answered Him, saying, "For a good work we do not stone You, but for blasphemy, and because You, being a Man, make Yourself God"* **(John 10:31-33 NKJV).**

And again, Jesus evaded them: *"Therefore they sought again to seize Him, but He escaped out of their hand"* (John 10:39 NKJV).

A report comes from Mary and Martha telling Jesus that His friend Lazarus is sick. John 11:5-8 (NLT) says:

So although Jesus loved Martha, Mary, and Lazarus, he stayed where he was for the next two days. Finally, he said to his disciples, "Let's go back to Judea." But his disciples objected. "Rabbi," they said, "only a few days ago the people in Judea were trying to stone you. Are you going there again?"

Were the disciples thinking about Lazarus or his sisters? No, they were thinking of their own lives. But Thomas, nicknamed the Twin, one of Jesus's disciples said, *"Let us also go, that we may die with Him"* (John 11:16 NKJV). Wow. Wouldn't you love to be around people like that?

"Oh pastor, oh friend. You're going off to a foreign land on a mission? Don't you know the dangers that lurk there? People are persecuted and killed for their faith daily. Even so, I will go with you. I know the anointing of God will protect and preserve us, even if it means we die together."

Then they took away the stone from the place where the dead man was lying. And Jesus lifted up His eyes and said, "Father, I thank You that You have heard Me. And I know that You always hear Me, but because of the people who are standing by I said this, that they may believe that You sent Me." Now when He had said these things, He cried with a loud voice, "Lazarus, come forth!" And he who had died came out bound hand and foot with graveclothes, and his face was wrapped with a cloth. Jesus said to them, "Loose him, and let him go" **(John 11:41-44 NKJV).**

Jesus brought Lazarus back from death to life—and now the religious leaders don't want to just kill Jesus, they want to kill Lazarus too (see John 12:10).

PROTECTION FROM THE EVIL ONE

Jesus says in John 17:15 (NIV), *"My prayer is not that you take them out of the world but that you protect them from the evil one."* We know that Jesus is coming again. I believe He is waiting for the end-time harvest that has not been fully reached and His church to arise gloriously. We are all looking forward to what He has promised before His return. He's coming for a glorious church. I think He deserves just that!

> *...Christ also loved the church and gave Himself for her, that He might sanctify and cleanse her with the washing of water by the word, that He might present her to Himself a glorious church, not having spot or wrinkle or any such thing, but that she should be holy and without blemish* **(Ephesians 5:25-27 NKJV).**

We should all want to make a difference in this world for the Lord by glorifying His name. I am eager to experience what it is like leading a church through times of revival. No one needs to flee in fear of a world gone wrong. We should not fear what's going on around us, instead we only fear the Lord. Remember we have been anointed with the anointing of preservation. His presence is our shield, and He will always keep us safe.

Jesus's prayer in the Garden of Gethsemane was concerning the future. He prayed, not to take them out of the world, but to *"protect them from the evil one."* What preserves us from evil? The anointing. It was still powerfully upon Jesus as He prayed from the time He announced it at the start of His ministry.

> *Jesus therefore, knowing all things that would come upon Him, went forward and said to them, "Whom are you seeking?" They answered Him, "Jesus of Nazareth." Jesus said to them, "I am He." And Judas, who betrayed Him, also stood with them. Now when He said to them, "I am He," they drew back and fell to the ground* (**John 18:4-6 NKJV**).

Jesus was praying in the Garden of Gethsemane, His presence so anointed and powerful that when He confessed His identity, everyone around Him fell to the ground in awe. It was a powerful moment.

Have you ever seen someone fall under the power of God? This is exactly what happened when they came to arrest Him! It was a powerful moment, as the anointing bestowed upon Jesus was so great that it caused everyone around Him to fall backward and lay on the ground as if they were dead. This was evidence of His supernatural protection and preservation, proving that no one could touch Him.

Before His crucifixion, Jesus performed a final miracle to prove the anointing that surrounded and preserved Him throughout His whole ministry. It was a powerful display of His divine power, showing that He was still in control even in such a difficult moment.

> But even as Jesus said this, a crowd approached, led by Judas, one of the twelve disciples. Judas walked over to Jesus to greet him with a kiss. But Jesus said, "Judas, would you betray the Son of Man with a kiss?" When the other disciples saw what was about to happen, they exclaimed, "Lord, should we fight? We brought the swords!" And one of them struck at the high priest's slave, slashing off his right ear. But Jesus said, "No more of this." And he touched the man's ear and healed him (Luke 22:47-51 NLT).

That anointing of preservation was still upon Jesus and I believe even intensified from His prayers in the Garden of Gethsemane that caused the man's ear to be reattached and totally healed! It was now time for that anointing that preserved Him to be lifted as He would now lay down His life for a ransom for many!

In John 18:11 (NKJV) Jesus says to Peter, "Put your sword into the sheath. Shall I not drink the cup which My Father has given Me?" In other words, Jesus knew His time had come, He had to lay down His life to fulfill God's will.

At that moment, the protection and anointing surrounding Jesus was removed. He was arrested and bound, something that had not been possible before due to His anointing from the Spirit of God. Knowing it was time for Him to make the ultimate sacrifice, Jesus let the anointing of preservation lift.

FOR A LONG LIFE...

I want to show you one last Scripture before closing this chapter. Proverbs 13:3 (NLT): *"**Those who control their tongue will have a long life**; opening your mouth can ruin everything."* As we can see from this Scripture, our mouths and our words determine preservation! It is a key to preserving your life and the anointing surrounding it is to decree it. Jesus used words at the start of His ministry proclaiming the anointing upon Him and at the end of His ministry opened His mouth saying the time had now come to lay His life down.

Let's continue using our words of faith by releasing God's anointing of preservation over ourselves, our families, our ministries, and even our nation. Never stop striving for a touch of His anointing of preservation in your life. This is wise; continue to watch what you say which helps maintain the anointing. Avoid negative talk as this compromises the anointing of preservation on your life.

9

LIMITLESS ANOINTING AND POWER

*But you have received **the Holy Spirit, and he lives within you**, so you don't need anyone to teach you what is true. For **the Spirit teaches you everything you need to know**, and what he teaches is true–it is not a lie. So just as he has taught you, **remain in fellowship with Christ*** (1 John 2:27 NLT).

Jesus's anointing of the Spirit was limitless, His glory immeasurable. This same anointing of preservation overshadowed Mary's womb when she carried Jesus and saved Him from an untimely death at the hands of an angry mob. It was this power that calmed the storms of life for His disciples, drowned demons, healed the lame man, the bleeding woman, and even a dead child.

We can access that same anointing power when we declare the truth of God's promises. We can increase our measure of His power when we remain connected and obedient to Him in prayer, declaring, "The Spirit of the Lord is upon me" every day.

BE BOLD!

It can be intimidating to go against the grain of what our current culture tells us, especially when some may push back or become angry. But we must have the boldness to stand firm in our declaration of God and His glory. We should not be deliberately rude or obnoxious, but our faith demands that we make ourselves heard—for Jesus.

Let us be bold and courageous in standing for God's values and morals and let us never forget to do so with grace. We should make it our daily prayer to stand before God's people and speak His truth—even if it means being a voice crying out in the wilderness. May we always strive to have the boldness that is accompanied by class.

That's what Jesus did.

Jesus was compassionate, loving, wise, patient, and even-tempered (except that time in the temple, see Matthew 21:12). But even so, Jesus made people angry—angry enough to make a crowd want to kill Him—which eventually happened.

The Bible reveals that from the beginning of John 7 all the way into the time of John 18, Jesus was criticized and hated for the truth He was preaching. Some sought to kill Him, some hated Him, others thought He was a deceiver, and He was even accused of being a demon. Yet in the three years Jesus walked upon the earth, no one could harm Him—until He knew His time had come and He willingly gave His life as a sacrifice for all people.

We must protect the anointing as Jesus did despite the onslaughts, accusations, and attempts to take His life. The anointing is a divinely appointed responsibility, a precious gift from God that enables us to accomplish His will for our lives.

The same anointing of preservation that upheld Jesus is available to us. Though there may be many enemies around and various unhealthy mandates, laws, rules, and regulations being imposed, God is protecting us and bringing us all through it with His special anointing of preservation.

During a time of war and turmoil, the young shepherd David was anointed with oil by God. This empowered him to take on a lion, bear, and even a giant warrior. David declared:

> You come to me with a sword, with a spear, and with a javelin. But I come to you in the name of the Lord of hosts, the God of the armies of Israel, whom you have defied. This day the Lord will deliver you into my hand, and I will strike you and take your head from you. And this day I will give the carcasses of the camp of the Philistines to the birds of the air and the wild beasts of the earth, that all the earth may know that there is a God in Israel. Then all this assembly shall know that the Lord does not save with sword and spear; for the battle is the Lord's, and He will give you into our hands (1 Samuel 17:45-47 NKJV).

After David's declaration, he *"put his hand in his bag and took out a stone; and he slung it and struck the Philistine in his forehead so that the stone sank into his forehead, and he fell on his face to the earth"* (1 Samuel 17:49 NKJV). His anointing of preservation protected him, and he killed the enemy.

I can recall the Lord's anointing on my life and watching how powerful feats of God kept me safe through many different circumstances—that is what the anointing is, it preserves us so we can fulfill God's will for us. The anointing is God's power on human flesh to do what human flesh alone could never do.

I remember that as the anointing in my life grew, I found myself able to do things that were previously impossible. I had been scared to preach; I was unable to talk in front of people, and even writing seemed a challenge. But due to the anointing, I was enabled to do all those things and so much more! The same is true for you as well because of the anointing of preservation.

AN EXCITING NEW ADVENTURE!

God will often ask us to do things we didn't think we could do. Think about David as a shepherd boy who had never faced a powerful warrior before, but the anointing of God on his life gave him victory. He didn't even need the armor that King Saul offered him to shield him from danger. David respectfully refused it, confident that the anointing of preservation would protect him in supernatural ways.

What can you do when anointed by the Spirit of God?

I never imagined I'd be married to such a beautiful, God-anointed woman, let alone have a ministry that impacts millions of people around the world. But that is my current reality—my life blessed by God's anointing. When He bestows His anointing on you, the same could happen in your life, marriage, children, business, and relationships. Believe me when I say that the anointing preserves and protects! I have seen it so many times not just in my life but in so many different circumstances.

God says in 1 Chronicles 16:22 and Psalm 105:15: *"Do not touch My anointed ones and do My prophets no harm."* Are you a Christian? Just the fact that you say you're a Christian, you are identifying with this truth, and the fact that you are anointed. Remember, as we discovered that the word "Christian" means anointed. So if you say, "I'm a Christian," you're saying, "The Spirit of the Lord is on me, I'm anointed."

God tells us not to impose our will upon His anointed church or cause any harm to His prophets. Why? Because the anointing preserves and protects them. When the enemy tries to interfere with God's work, they are dealt with by the Lord, and those He has blessed are kept safe and secure.

EVIL FIRE HAS NO POWER

King Nebuchadnezzar saw firsthand the power of the anointing of preservation when he tried to force three Hebrew young men to worship an idol. The king said:

> *"...But if you do not worship, you shall be cast immediately into the midst of a burning fiery furnace. And who is the god who will deliver you from my hands?"*
>
> *Shadrach, Meshach, and Abed-Nego answered and said to the king, "O Nebuchadnezzar, we have no need to answer you in this matter. If that is the case, our God whom we serve is able to deliver us from the burning fiery furnace, and He will deliver us from your hand, O king. But if not, let it be known to you, O king, that we do not serve your gods, nor will we worship the gold image which you have set up."*
>
> *Then Nebuchadnezzar was full of fury, and the expression on his face changed toward Shadrach, Meshach, and Abed-Nego. He spoke and commanded that they heat the furnace seven times more than it was usually heated. And he commanded certain mighty men of valor who were in his army to bind Shadrach, Meshach, and Abed-Nego, and cast them into the burning fiery furnace. Then these men were bound in their coats, their trousers, their turbans, and their other garments, and were*

cast into the midst of the burning fiery furnace. Therefore, because the king's command was urgent, and the furnace exceedingly hot, the flame of the fire killed those men who took up Shadrach, Meshach, and Abed-Nego. And these three men, Shadrach, Meshach, and Abed-Nego, fell down bound into the midst of the burning fiery furnace.

Then King Nebuchadnezzar was astonished; and he rose in haste and spoke, saying to his counselors, "Did we not cast three men bound into the midst of the fire?" They answered and said to the king, "True, O king." "Look!" he answered, "I see four men loose, walking in the midst of the fire; and they are not hurt, and the form of the fourth is like the Son of God."

Then Nebuchadnezzar went near the mouth of the burning fiery furnace and spoke, saying, "Shadrach, Meshach, and Abed-Nego, servants of the Most High God, come out, and come here." Then Shadrach, Meshach, and Abed-Nego came from the midst of the fire. And the satraps, administrators, governors, and the king's counselors gathered together, and they saw these men on whose bodies the fire had no power; the hair of their head was not singed nor were their garments affected, and the smell of fire was not on them (Daniel 3:15-27 NKJV).

God's powerful anointing preserved them and kept them in that place of the anointing. And God received all His deserved glory!

The power comes through the blood of Jesus. The power of God comes through the Holy Spirit, Acts 10:38 (NKJV) says, *"God anointed Jesus of Nazareth with the Holy Spirit and with power...."* So part of the power you have is not just authority, it's a spiritual privilege or state of the anointing. When the anointing of God is on you and you declare it, you then have the same power that Jesus was anointed with to tread upon serpents and scorpions and over all the powers of the devil. That by no means shall anything harm or injure you. (See Psalm 91:10-13; Luke 10:19.)

Why are you untouchable? Because the power of the anointing protects you. What is this power derived from? The Holy Spirit and His blessing. It is called spiritual and natural immunity! Jesus said *by no means,* well that means nothing in the natural and spiritual realm. We find this further truth and benefit once again in Psalm 121 that are our blood covenant rights along with the anointing of preservation that preserves our lives from all evil.

The Lord shall preserve thee from all evil: he shall preserve thy soul (**Psalm 121:7 KJV**).

All means all and nothing means nothing. This is what we need to connect our faith to. It is our right and privilege provided for us in our covenant with almighty God to be preserved from evil. What can ruin that protection, leaving your life open to trouble? Allowing "flies"—any negativity or interference—to contaminate what you are doing. Let's not also forget we must give no place to the devil as he is called the lord of the flies. When we do, we attract them to our lives to hinder the anointing of preservation.

Ecclesiastes 10:1 (NKJV) says:

> *Dead flies putrefy the perfumer's ointment, and cause it to give off a foul odor; so does a little folly to one respected for wisdom and honor.*

In other words, flies will negatively change the dynamics of the anointing. So, my questions are: Why would we ever let flies enter a no-fly zone, and why would we ever let flies come in and mess with our houses, our bodies, our cars, our marriages, our kids, and our finances? We must establish a no-fly zone standard, or as the Scripture we read in Ecclesiastes says, will hinder the anointing of preservation if we don't.

"Shoo fly, don't bother me!"

What do I mean by a no-fly zone?

To better explain, a no-fly zone is likened to when the children of Israel had no flies in their homes, but the Egyptians did. There was an anointing of preservation that preserved them, thus establishing a no-fly zone. Not one fly was seen among them. We need to do as that old, well-known song, "Shoo fly, don't bother me!"

Now let's look at Ecclesiastes 9:8 (NKJV) which says, *"Let your garments always be white...."* The Amplified Version says it this way, *"Let your clothes always be white [with purity]...."* Your lifestyle is reflected in your clothing, which should be as clean as possible.

We must not adapt the mindset that we can do what we want because we are forgiven. When you are born again, you become righteous in the eyes of God. This is your spiritual status, but to receive the abundance promised by Jesus, you must also make healthy choices in your everyday life as that is your living standard or lifestyle. This includes avoiding any interference from negative influences like "flies."

PSALM 23—NOT JUST FOR FUNERALS

By living according to God's standards, you have the power to take advantage of the fullness of life. I want to show you a powerful truth from Scripture that is usually used regarding funerals, but a powerful Psalm of preservation!

Let's read it before we get into why the Lord kept bringing this Psalm to my mind lately:

> *The Lord is my shepherd;*
> *I shall not want.*

He makes me to lie down in green pastures;
He leads me beside the still waters.
He restores my soul;
He leads me in the paths of righteousness for His
name's sake.
Yea, though I walk through the valley of the
shadow of death,
I will fear no evil; for You are with me;
Your rod and Your staff, they comfort me.
You prepare a table before me in the presence of
my enemies;
You anoint my head with oil; my cup runs over.
Surely goodness and mercy shall follow me all
the days of my life;
and I will dwell in the house of the Lord forever
(Psalm 23 NKJV).

If Psalm 23 is a Scripture that resonates with you, there is nothing wrong with requesting it to be read at your own funeral. It is important to understand, however, that despite referring to the "shadow of death," it is not implicitly speaking of funerals; the psalmist walked through the valley, but never reached its end.

Sometimes when I am studying the Word and spending time with the Holy Spirit, He keeps nudging me. One time He kept saying, "Go over to Psalm 23."

I didn't want to go to Psalm 23, because it wasn't making any sense with what I was studying.

But He kept pushing on me, "Go to Psalm 23."

Eventually, I responded to the Holy Spirit and said, "I will do it," though it took me some time. As I opened to Psalm 23 in my Bible, His voice spoke to me, "Hank, this psalm is one of preservation."

"It is?"

He said, "It's a psalm of preservation and it's connected to the anointing."

"Okay, Lord, lead the way."

So here we go in Psalm 23:

"The Lord is my Shepherd. I shall want." I will have no lack of any good thing. So if you never lack, it means your life is preserved in a blessing of prosperity.

"He makes me..." Notice the wording is not suggestive. If He's really your Shepherd, then whatever He says goes. That's why Jesus says in Luke 6:46, *"Why do you call Me 'Lord, Lord' and not do the things which I say?"* Our life is gloriously blessed and preserved when we let the Lord lead, guide, and provide!

The psalm continues, *"He makes me to lie down in green pastures."* That's a place of feeding, a place of blessing and preservation because there is provision as seen in the green pastures and not some barren land. *"He leads me beside the still waters."* Do you know what's good about that? That's preservation. He's taking away all the rough waters, all the bad news, all the doom and gloom.

"He restores my soul; He leads me in the paths of righteousness for His name's sake. Yea, though I walk through the valley of the shadow of death..." This says that though we walk through what appears or looks like and feels like

it could be death, it's just a shadow. Think about how that has applied to what many have recently walked through on earth. We are to fear no evil for He is with us! Why? We are preserved.

"I will fear no evil; for You are with me; Your rod and Your staff, they comfort me." The anointed One is always with us. His anointing protects us, and the very rod and staff He uses is for the purpose of preservation!

"You prepare a table before me in the presence of my enemies." God set the table of blessing, healing, wholeness, prosperity, deliverance, preservation, and protection, all spread out just for you. We are to celebrate what Jesus did for us. He said, "Do this in remembrance of Me."

"You anoint my head with oil; my cup runs over." You're anointed and preserved because of it. And not only are you anointed, but you also ought to live a life where that anointing is dripping all over everyone who knows you. Why? Because you're constantly declaring, "The Spirit of the Lord is upon me. The Spirit of the Lord is supporting and protecting me. I'm anointed. I'm anointed with power and with preservation!"

"Surely goodness and mercy shall follow me all the days of my life." God's goodness and mercy are miraculous and take priority over make-believe fears and threats. My life is anointed with goodness and God's mercy blesses me every day. I'm anointed. I'm preserved. The news of the day will not affect me because I'm dripping with anointing.

"And I will dwell in the house of the Lord forever." Heaven is waiting for all believers, but in the meantime, we can

dwell in His house, as He lives within us. The apostle Paul tells us in 1 Corinthians 6:19-20, *"Or do you not know that **your body is the temple of the Holy Spirit** who is in you, whom you have from God, and you are not your own? For you were bought at a price; **therefore glorify God in your body and in your spirit**, which are God's."*

ABIDING IN GOD'S SHADOW

As we close this last chapter of the book, I urge you to prayerfully read the following psalm and absorb it into your heart, spirit, and mind. Take comfort in all the truth declared in Psalm 91 (NLT):

> *Those who live in the shelter of the Most High*
> *will find rest in the shadow of the Almighty.*
> *This I declare about the Lord:*
> *He alone is my refuge, my place of safety;*
> *he is my God, and I trust him.*
> *For he will rescue you from every trap*
> *and protect you from deadly disease.*
> *He will cover you with his feathers.*
> *He will shelter you with his wings.*
> *His faithful promises are your armor and protection.*
> *Do not be afraid of the terrors of the night,*
> *nor the arrow that flies in the day.*
> *Do not dread the disease that stalks in darkness,*
> *nor the disaster that strikes at midday.*

Though a thousand fall at your side,
though ten thousand are dying around you,
these evils will not touch you.
Just open your eyes,
and see how the wicked are punished.
If you make the Lord your refuge,
if you make the Most High your shelter,
no evil will conquer you;
no plague will come near your home.
For he will order his angels
to protect you wherever you go.
They will hold you up with their hands
so you won't even hurt your foot on a stone.
You will trample upon lions and cobras;
you will crush fierce lions and serpents under
your feet!
The Lord says, "I will rescue those who love me.
I will protect those who trust in my name.
When they call on me, I will answer;
I will be with them in trouble.
I will rescue and honor them.
I will reward them with a long life
and give them my salvation.

This psalm applies to circumstances today in our nation and in our homes. Many people—believers and unbelievers alike—are restless, unsettled, and agitated. Taking Him as a refuge will help us to better manage our apprehensions about the state of our nation and the tumultuous times we are facing.

The enemy is actively trying to ensnare us through the various media platforms available to him. He plants seeds of doubt in our hearts, aiming to lead us away from believing in God's Word. But thanks be to Him—He has promised to shield and protect us from all evil!

Wrapped in the embrace of God's wings and armored by His protection, we can find peace, preservation, and safety that only He can provide. There is a special anointing connected to these wings that can heal our troubles. So let us seek the sanctuary of His wings and cling fast to the promises of His restoration.

BELIEVE AND CLING TO HIS PROMISE OF HEALING.

As a beloved child of the Father, you do not need to fear threats by night or day. For under His wings and anointing, no bug, pestilence, nor destructive force can touch you. Under God's protection, you are sheltered and will be kept safe. This is all because He has anointed you with an anointing that preserves and keeps those who trust in Him, His Word, and promises.

Though thousands may perish around you, no evil shall befall you. It can't! Why? You are gloriously preserved with an anointing of preservation that preserves your coming in, in between, and your going out! You will witness the wicked meet their justice and you will take refuge in God. Secure in His shelter, no plague shall come near you or your family. Embrace His love; He will save and guard those who put their faith in Him.

The last two verses of Psalm 91 say that God will answer your prayers and He will be with you in trouble—rescuing you and honoring you when you call on Him. And He will reward you with a long life and give you His salvation for eternity. All this is preservation and is available and activated as we claim it and decree it.

I believe you have been encouraged as you have read this book and the anointing of preservation has become a reality. I want to pray and release the anointing over everyone who ever reads this book. I believe as a result that yokes are destroyed and burdens are removed, and devils are driven out in the name of Yeshua. I urge you to keep declaring, "I am anointed, for the Spirit of the Lord is upon me and I receive that anointing of preservation and release it over my loved ones and this nation."

I release that anointing into your life for your loved ones. I decree that anointing over you of the Holy Spirit destroys every yoke of sicknesses, the yoke of disease, pain, and burdens. I speak forth the anointing to break and destroy witchcraft, voodoo, and spirits of divination. The anointing of the Holy Spirit destroys every yoke of the devil, every yoke of the curse of anxiety and fear; there will be no cancer, no dementia, no Alzheimer's, no bipolar, no mental disorders or diseases or losses, no disease, no infirmity, no pain or calamities, destruction or tragedy. I speak and declare the anointing of preservation upon you in a greater way than ever before.

I wholeheartedly believe while reading this book, you have received the anointing of preservation and have come into greater revelation concerning it. Now, I encourage you to continue declaring it and releasing it. Remember, the Spirit of the Lord is upon you, you are anointed! Therefore you are preserved!

YOUR PERSONAL INVITATION

If you've never decided to follow Jesus Christ as your personal Savior, if you aren't sure if you will enter Heaven after you die, God can give you the positive assurance right now that you can be a member of God's family and spend eternity in Heaven.

As the very first chapter in this book revealed, your words are powerful. The Bible, God's Word, acknowledges your power as it says in Romans 10:9-10 (NIV), *"If you declare with your mouth, 'Jesus is Lord,' and believe in your heart that God raised him from the dead, you will be saved. For it is with your heart that you believe and are justified, and it is with your mouth that you profess your faith and are saved."*

If you're not 100 percent sure that you are saved by the blood of Jesus, all you have to do is make that decision in your heart, profess it with your mouth, and pray this prayer out loud:

"Father, in the name of Jesus, I thank You. Thank You for sending Your Son Jesus to earth to die for me. Thank You for forgiving me of my sins. I believe that Jesus went to the cross and died, was buried, and on the third day He rose from the dead and now sits with You in Heaven. Jesus, I accept You into my life. On this day, right now, I accept You as my Savior and I'll serve You all the days of my life, in Jesus's name. Amen."

Welcome to the family of God!

Regardless of where you are today, continue to go after the Lord! Press in to be closer than you ever have before by adding the baptism of the Holy Spirit to your life. I have included the means to add to your anointing of preservation by offering you a brief instruction on how to receive His precious baptism and also how to minister to others—both of which are also found in my book, *The Supernatural Power of Jesus' Blood—Applying the Blessings Available Through Jesus' Blood:*

RECEIVING AND MINISTERING THE BAPTISM OF THE HOLY SPIRIT

The following are several simple steps you can use to receive, or help someone else to receive, the baptism of the

Holy Spirit. These steps are patterned after the way people received in the book of Acts.

1. **Make sure they are a Christian and they have made Jesus their Lord and Savior.**

We must be saved before we can receive the baptism of the Holy Spirit. For many, it is helpful to ask them if they are sure they are saved. Some struggle to receive simply because they are not sure they are even right with God.

2. **Encourage them that this is a biblical promise God wants them to have.**

In Acts 2:38-39, Peter encouraged the hearers on the Day of Pentecost that this promise was for them and their children, and it is still for us today (see James 1:17; Heb. 13:8).

3. **Let them know they are receiving the Holy Spirit, not just tongues.**

Speaking in tongues is only the evidence of the Holy Spirit filling them. However, the focus is the Holy Spirit and His power filling their life, not speaking in tongues only.

4. **Lead them in a prayer.**

Truthfully, in most scriptural examples, people didn't pray an actual prayer to receive, but they did need to exercise their faith and be expectant to receive. Often repeating a prayer helps people use their faith for receiving. Remember, God always answers the heart that seeks Him, and He delights in answering our prayers!

5. Pray for them and lay hands on them.

If you are alone, you can still receive the baptism of the Holy Spirit! You can simply lay hands on yourself and tell the Lord you want to receive. If you're with someone else, you may want to lay your hands on them and pray for them to receive and gently say, "Receive the Holy Spirit." In the Bible, we find the disciples laying hands on the recipients. However, in some cases they did not. The Holy Spirit just fell on them.

6. Tell them to expect to speak in tongues.

Some people are more confident and will instantly start speaking out in tongues. Others need encouraging. Remember that although the Holy Spirit forms the language, *they* have to do the talking. It often helps to have them open their mouth and move their tongue and stop any speaking in their natural language. Sometimes people will hear unusual syllables or sounds in their heart or mind. Tell them to speak them out without worrying how they sound. It helps if you also start speaking in tongues along with them.

If you are alone and praying to receive for yourself, you should also expect to speak in tongues. Use the above steps as a guideline—open your mouth, move your tongue, and stop speaking in your natural language. As you yield yourself to the Lord, speak out any unusual sounds or syllables without worrying what you sound like.

OVERCOMING ANY FEARS ABOUT THE BAPTISM OF THE HOLY SPIRIT

Here are a few common questions some people may have about the baptism of the Holy Spirit and corresponding answers that can be helpful to share:

1. Can I accidentally receive a "wrong" or "evil spirit" instead of the Holy Spirit?

You don't have to worry about getting a "wrong" spirit or a demon instead of the Holy Spirit. Luke 11 says:

> *If a son shall ask bread of any of you that is a father, will he give him a stone? or if he ask a fish, will he for a fish give him a serpent? Or if he shall ask an egg, will he offer him a scorpion? If ye then, being evil, know how to give good gifts unto your children; how much more shall your heavenly Father give the Holy Spirit to them that ask him?* (Luke 11:11-13 KJV).

2. What if I don't speak in tongues?

If you don't seem to "hear" any syllables in your heart, be bold enough to just move your mouth and make sounds. Isaiah 28:11 says, *"For with stammering lips and another tongue will he speak to this people."* The experience is different for everyone, so if your lips just seem to babble or stammer at first, this is okay. Remember every person's experience may not be the same!

3. Are the tongues fake or just in my mind?

Remember that when you speak in tongues, it is you who does the speaking, while the Holy Spirit gives the utterance. Acts 19:6 (KJV) says, *"and they spake with tongues."* Who spoke? They did! Yes, it will sound like you, and you will hear the words in your mind too, while the Holy Spirit is forming those sounds into a powerful and supernatural language!

STRONG SPIRIT, STRONG LIFE

Most of us are very familiar with our natural minds being in control, so allowing your spirit to be in control as you pray in tongues will take some practice. Don't get discouraged—the more you do it, the more you are building up your spirit and before you know it, it will be second nature to you.

As we strengthen our spirits, we allow them to rule over our souls (mind, will, and emotions). You may find your spirit gaining victories over the battles you used to fight in your mind, your will, and your emotions. Now, you might not feel anything or notice this immediately, but over time you will be strengthened, joyful, and full of faith. When our spirits are strong, our faith is built up and we are confident that God will work miracles both within us and for others as we minister to them. Like the disciples, we will go forth empowered as the Lord's witnesses, taking the Gospel to the ends of the earth with signs, wonders, and miracles!

ABOUT
HANK KUNNEMAN

Hank Kunneman pastors Lord of Hosts Church in Omaha, Nebraska, with his wife, Brenda. Together they host a weekly program, "New Level with Hank and Brenda," which can be watched on their own network One Voice TV, as well as on The Victory Channel, and Daystar Television Network. As an author and uncompromising voice for God's Word, Hank is known for a strong prophetic anointing, preaching, and ministering in meetings and on national television programs. His ministry has truly been marked for accuracy in national and worldwide events.

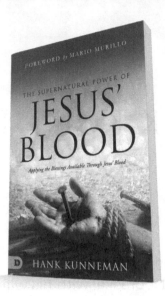

From

Hank Kunneman

Receive the Father's heart and understand the power of Throne Room prophecy!

When it comes to prophecy, how can we discern if the words being spoken are true, false, or wrong? God is calling His people to press into a higher realm of revelation, so that the words they share come from Heaven, *not* from their flesh, soul, or other sources.

Hank Kunneman is a trusted father and mentor in the prophetic community. In this landmark book, he teaches you to speak prophetic words that carry thunder from Heaven's Throne Room! Learn to communicate messages from God with precision and accuracy—carrying the Father's heart as you carry His secrets.

In this timely book you will learn...

•To discern the three realms of information—the Earth realm, the occult realm, and the Throne Room realm.
•How prophetic words are important in the course of world events, in times of crisis, and in challenging times.
•To draw closer to the One seated on the Throne to increase intimacy necessary for prophetic accuracy.
•How "human filters" affect every prophet and prophecy.
•How to identify the characteristics of false *"horned"* prophets.

Now is the time to come up higher and receive the Father's heart and understand the power of Throne Room prophecy!

Purchase your copy wherever books are sold

From

Brenda Kunneman

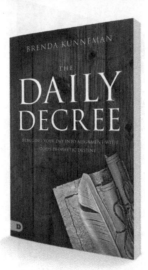

Proclaim the words of the Lord!

There are words from Heaven that the King of kings wants you to decree! Like Jesus, believers must listen for the Father's voice and declare what He has spoken. When you boldly decree God's word, your words are saturated in the supernatural life and creative power of the Kingdom!

Respected prophetic voice Brenda Kunneman has compiled a series of powerful decrees that were birthed in the heart of God, shared with her, and now imparted to you. These legal decrees will empower you with tools to overcome impossibilities, position you for new levels of blessing, and prepare you for supernatural encounters.

Declare the words of the King, and claim His promises today!

Purchase your copy wherever books are sold.

From

BRENDA KUNNEMAN

Decree your victory and defeat hell's schemes against your family!

In an age where our families are under attack from all sides, you have a sure strategy to secure Heaven's victory over your marriage, children, and household: boldly decree the Word of God!

Bestselling author and dynamic prophetic voice Brenda Kunneman has equipped believers around the world to decree Heaven's victory over every area of their lives. In *Daily Decrees for Family Blessing and Breakthrough*, she empowers you with powerful, Bible-based prophetic declarations to overcome every strategy of the enemy that comes against your marriage, your children, your finances, and your household.

Take authority over your family! Don't let the devil win another victory. Rise up with the Word of God on your lips and decree Heaven's promises over every area of your family life!

Purchase your copy wherever books are sold.

YOUR Prophetic COMMUNITY